1,001
Ways to
Celebrate

Family

& Create Lasting
Memories

1,001
Ways to
Celebrate

Family

& Create Lasting
Memories

CIDER MILL
PRESS

BOOK
PUBLISHERS
KENNEBUNKPORT, MAINE

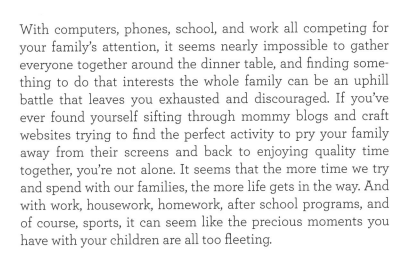

With computers, phones, school, and work all competing for your family's attention, it seems nearly impossible to gather everyone together around the dinner table, and finding something to do that interests the whole family can be an uphill battle that leaves you exhausted and discouraged. If you've ever found yourself sifting through mommy blogs and craft websites trying to find the perfect activity to pry your family away from their screens and back to enjoying quality time together, you're not alone. It seems that the more time we try and spend with our families, the more life gets in the way. And with work, housework, homework, after school programs, and of course, sports, it can seem like the precious moments you have with your children are all too fleeting.

Family used to be the uniting force from which everything else stemmed. Now, with today's work schedules and the steadily increasing time children spend at school or on the computer, trying to fight for a few precious minutes of time together can be overwhelming.

If the idea of trying to plan your next family activity has you discouraged and wondering if you should simply give up, think again! From unplugged activities centered around giving back to the community to scavenger hunts, crafts, recipes, and more, all aimed at creating quality memories that will last a lifetime, this book is sure to get you excited to plan your next family outing. You can use these family-friendly activities as guidelines and tailor them for what works best for you and yours, or treat them like a bucket list of family fun—after all, there are over 1,000 of them to choose from! And for those looking for a quick game, recipe, or craft to boost their family togetherness, there are plenty of 5-minute activities in here that will create laughter, bring you closer together, and add a sprinkle of family joy to help you all feel connected.

If you're feeling adventurous, use these activities as a step-by-step list of what to do next, or you can simply flip to a random page and pick out your activity for the day. Just like spending time together as a family, there's no real wrong way to use this book. So choose an activity, plan your next grand adventure, and celebrate family like never before.

1

Play dinosaur tag. Whoever is "it" has to scrunch their arms into their t-shirt to make their arms short like a *T. rex* and try and tag people.

2

Go berry picking at a local farm. Remember to eat while you pick!

3

Jump into a lake on a hot summer day.

4

Plan a go-kart racing trip. If you're feeling adventurous, have everyone dress up as their favorite Mario Kart characters.

5

Write new words to one of your family's favorite songs, then sing it as a group.

6

Pretend that the floor has turned to lava. If you don't like the idea of everyone running over the furniture, you can set out pillows and blankets to jump on instead.

7

Make thumbprint dandelions or fingerprint flowers and hang them all over your house.

8

Take your scooters to a local skate park or teach your kids how to skateboard.

9

Host a make-your-own-pizza party, complete with a topping bar and different kinds of dough. Don't forget dessert pizzas!

10

Go for a color run. If running isn't your kids' style, they can always join in for the last leg of the race.

11

Blindfold the kids and go for a drive. When you arrive at your destination, have them remove their blindfolds and instruct you on how to get back home. This is also a great way to teach map reading skills.

12

Paint with colored ice cubes. Simply mix washable watercolors and water in an ice tray and freeze overnight, then use them to decorate card stock as they melt.

13

Buy a new notebook and fill it as a family. You can sketch, doodle, color, or even scrapbook!

14

Make a gift for your local sanitation worker. It's always a great idea to show appreciation for the people who help keep our towns clean.

15

Make edible play dough.

Ingredients

2 cups water
2½ cups white flour, plus more for dusting
½ cup salt
1 tablespoon cream of tartar
2 (0.13 oz.) packages unsweetened, fruit-flavored soft drink mix
3 tablespoons vegetable oil

Directions

· Add the water to a saucepan and bring to a boil. Remove from heat and set aside.

· Whisk together the flour, salt, cream of tartar, and soft drink mix in a large bowl. Stir the vegetable oil into the flour mixture using a spoon. Pour the hot water in the bowl and continue stirring.

· When the dough is cool enough to handle, lightly flour a flat surface and knead the dough until smooth and elastic, about 8 minutes. Store in the refrigerator when not using.

16
Play who am I?

Tools
  Markers
  Index cards
  Large rubber bands or headbands
  Timer

How to play:
- Write out as many animals, objects, and people you can think of, keeping to one per each index card. Make sure to shuffle them.

- Give each player a rubber band or headband.

- Each player draws an index card without looking at it and puts it in their headband.

- Start the timer for 30 seconds. Each player can ask as many yes or no questions about their index card as they can ask in 30 seconds, and the remaining players have to answer truthfully. If they guess what their card is, they can draw another index card and guess that one as well. Once the timer runs out, switch to the next person.

- At the end of three to five rounds, whoever has the most correctly guessed cards wins.

Santa Claus

17

Make a family tree. You can either stick with a simple design on a piece of paper or make a full-fledged tree to hang up in your living room, complete with pictures.

18

Play telephone.

19

Designate one night of the week as a themed dress-up dinner night. You can all dress up as royalty or wear your scariest Halloween costumes.

20

Build a model airplane together. Make sure to choose an easier model if you have younger kids.

21

Grab your camera and go on an outdoor photo hunt. Make the objects you're looking for line up with the time of year for a fun, seasonal activity.

22

Have an egg drop contest. Each family member makes a protective casing for an egg using recyclable materials. See which designs keep the eggs safest when dropped from high up.

23

Go to a local outdoor concert. Many towns offer free attendance, making this a great way to spend a cool summer night.

24

Cover your dining table with craft paper and paint a giant collaborative mural. If you want, you can all draw something following the same theme, like, "Our favorite games" or, "What we love about fall."

25

Hold an international candy sampling night. You can find plenty of international candies for sale online. You might even find a new favorite treat!

26

Decorate a pumpkin this fall and enter it into a local contest or have your own contest!

27

Make refrigerator magnets. You can easily pick up magnets at your local craft store and use air-dry clay to make animals, shapes, or robots.

28

Create a fort out of blankets in your living room. Try and see if you can fill the whole living room with your new hangout spot!

29

Have your kids put on a magic show, complete with musical cues.

30

Visit a laser lights show.

31

Make candied apples.

Ingredients

2 cups granulated sugar
½ cup light corn syrup
¾ cup water
2 to 3 drops red food coloring
4 Popsicle sticks
4 apples

Directions

- Place the sugar, corn syrup, and water in a medium saucepan and cook over high heat, swirling a few times.

- When the syrup begins to boil, lower the heat to medium-high and continue to boil for approximately 20 minutes, until a candy thermometer reads just over 300°F. Remove from heat. Stir in the food coloring.

- Insert Popsicle sticks into the apples and dip them into the syrup, turning to ensure they are completed coated. Set the candy-coated apples on a lightly greased baking sheet and let stand until the candy shell is hard.

Make a pom-pom shooter.

Tools
Plastic cup
Balloon
Clear tape
Pom-poms

Directions
- Cut the bottom off of the plastic cup and tie a knot in the bottom of the uninflated balloon. Cut the top off of the balloon and wrap around the top of the cup, taping it in place so you have a hollow space to place your pom-poms.

- To launch the pom-poms, pull back the knotted balloon end and then let go to send the pom-poms flying.

TO US, FAMILY
YOUR ARMS
OTHER AND

MEANS PUTTING
AROUND EACH
BEING THERE.

—Barbara Bush

33

Use white tissues, a black marker, and rubber bands to make miniature ghosts. Hang them in your windows for some spooky fun.

34

Investigate your yard with a magnifying glass. Keep a list going of all the cool creatures and plants you find, as well as any lost buttons or toys.

35

Play leapfrog.

36

Have a glow-in-the-dark party, complete with glow-in-the-dark bracelets, face paint, and arts and crafts.

37

Play hot potato.

38

Have a campfire singalong. Be sure to include favorites like "Down by the Bay" and "The Lion Sleeps Tonight."

39

Nothing says family time like great manners. Take an etiquette class as a family and then put your new manners to the test at a dinner party with friends.

40

Go to the beach and hunt for shark teeth. Then, turn them into necklaces or keep them in a mason jar.

41

Write messages as a family using sparklers and the long exposure setting on your camera.

42

Leave gifts at your neighbor's doorstep and hide to watch their response.

43

Do yoga together as a family. Try easy poses like Downward Dog or Child Pose to get you started.

44

Write encouraging letters to each other and then mail them three months later for a wholesome surprise.

45

Go stair sledding with pillows, mattresses, and sleeping bags. Make sure to pad the edges of your railing with extra pillows to avoid any bumps.

46

Interview each family member on video asking a short list of questions (favorite memory from the year, favorite family activity, etc.) and put all the answers into an end-of-the-year appreciation video.

47

When Halloween rolls around, decorate each other's trick-or-treat bags with spooky faces.

Make root beer floats.

Ingredients
1 pint vanilla ice cream
Root beer, as needed
Whipped cream, for topping

Directions
- Place two scoops of the ice cream at the bottom of each glass. Slowly pour the root beer into the glass to prevent foaming, then top with whipped cream and serve.

Play would you rather.

How to play:

- Have one person be the question asker. The rest of the family gathers in the center of the room. Designate one side of the room as one answer to the question, and the other side of the room as the second answer.

- The question asker asks the group to choose between two options, and each person runs to the side they would rather pick. They then explain why they picked that option to the group. Remember: there's no sitting down in the center of the room if you can't decide!

50

Make your own family board game. Let the kids come up with the rules to help teach them about fairness.

51

Have a pillow fight.

52

Make nature faces out of outdoor supplies like leaves and twigs, then hang them up in the living room to celebrate spring.

53

Play post office at home. Make your own mailboxes and write letters to each other using specific addresses like, "Mom, in the study" or, "Tommy, on the front porch."

54

Make homemade paper dolls, complete with outfits. It's easiest to cut out the doll body first, then trace it onto a fresh sheet of paper and draw clothes that way.

55

Play pickleball.

56

Make a comic book together. You can make a superhero story about your family, or chronicle one of your latest family adventures.

57

Visit a science museum, and don't be surprised if you end up enjoying the visit as much as the kids!

58

Make your own "stained glass" drawings with markers, crayons, and wax paper. Draw the outline of what you want to draw in marker, then color it in with crayons and hang it in the window for a colorful surprise!

59

Play follow-the-leader.

60

Start a paint-by-numbers project. Each family member can be in charge of a different color, or you can have a race to see who can finish their project first.

61

Write a family bucket list and do something on it together.

62

Hit up your local garden, park, forest, or yard to collect items for a terrarium. Then, add everything you find to a mason jar.

63

Have a sponge fight in the driveway. Once everyone is sopping wet, add some soap and wash the family car!

64

Order pizzas from all over town and judge which is the best.

65

Go apple picking at an orchard.

REJOICE WITH THE BEAUTIFUL

YOUR FAMILY IN LAND OF LIFE.

—Albert Einstein

66

Visit an animal shelter as a family and pick out a new pet.

67

Have an at-home spelling bee, complete with a stuffed animal audience. You can find old lists of National Spelling Bee questions online or make up your own list. Here are a few to get you started: sassafras, onomatopoeia, neighborhood, receipt, delicious.

68

Make glow-in-the-dark snow monsters by building snowmen and putting glow sticks in their eyes or around their arms for a spooky nighttime surprise.

69

If anyone in your family wears glasses, have everyone take turns wearing different glasses and see if they can do basic tasks like reading instructions or finding the remote. Be careful if the glasses have a very strong prescription, as you could give yourself a headache!

70

Start a food blog for your family dinners, but let your kids write the posts and food reviews.

71

Learn a clapping game like Miss Mary Mack and see how fast you can go.

12

Make your own texture book from recycled fabrics. Using a ruled notebook, let each kid pick out things they like the texture of and turn them into their own touch-and-feel book. If they're feeling adventurous, have them come up with a story using all their textures.

13

Place a sprinkler under the trampoline or add water balloons for high-flying summer fun!

14

Go to the barber shop or salon together. Be sure to pamper yourselves with a shampoo or a nice shave (with just shaving cream for the kids, of course).

15

Make cars and a car track from rocks found in the backyard and a little bit of paint. Be sure to weatherproof them so they last longer.

16

Jump in rain puddles.

17

Make a family calendar together. You can include things like birthdays, family holidays, or even your favorite memories, like the one-year anniversary of when you adopted your family pet.

18

Play capture the flag.

Make a kaleidoscope.

Tools

Paper towel roll
Scissors
Aluminum foil
White card stock
Clear tape
Plastic berry container
Hot glue gun
Colorful plastic beads
Corrugated scrapbook paper

Directions

- Measure the paper towel roll and cut a piece of aluminum foil and white card stock to be 1½ inches shorter than the length of the roll. Tape the aluminum foil to the card stock, keeping the foil as flat as possible. This will be your mirror. Cut the aluminum foil and card stock to the width of the inside of the roll by measuring the diameter of the roll, dividing in half, and then multiplying by three. Score the aluminum foil in three even lines, then fold into a triangle and tape, keeping the aluminum foil side facing inward.

- Trace the end of your paper towel roll and cut three circles from the plastic container at this size. Place one of the circles on the end of the roll and hot glue into place. Insert the mirror triangle into the roll so it rests on the plastic surface. Turn over your tube and insert the second circle of plastic inside the tube so it rests on the end of the mirror and glue in place.

- Add the colorful beads so they rest on the interior piece of plastic. Secure the last piece of plastic on the remaining open end of the roll.

- To make the spinner, take the corrugated scrapbook paper and cut so it is ½ the length of the roll. Then, wrap around the roll and secure the long edges using tape so the tube of paper can spin around the paper towel tube.

- If desired, cut a circle out of the remaining white card stock with a small hole in the center for the eyepiece. Tape onto the end of the tube that is farthest from the beads to finish the kaleidoscope.

80

Plant fall flowers.

81

Make a tinfoil mosaic using tissue paper, glue, and a piece of card stock. Have your kids draw the outline they want to fill in, then use the tinfoil and tissue paper to color in different areas by rolling them into small pieces and gluing them to the paper. You can also use leftover holiday wrapping paper for this project.

82

Donate old toys or books to your local thrift store.

83

Play with a jumbo parachute in the back yard.

84

Go on an alphabet treasure hunt and see if you can find things in nature that begin with every letter of the alphabet.

85

Have a not-so-extreme home makeover. You could always paint a hallway, or just rearrange some furniture in the living room.

86

Have a library trip where everyone is assigned another family member. They have to pick out a book they think their assigned family member would like and check it out for them.

87

Make your own themed family Halloween costumes. Be sure to take a photo!

88

Have a relay race. You can make this as serious or as silly as you'd like. If you have older kids, up the difficulty by making it a backward or blindfolded relay race.

89

Play pin the tail on the donkey.

90

Learn about Eid al-Fitr and talk about how forgiveness and community are a big part of the holiday.

91

Paint with bubbles by mixing washable watercolors and soapy water together. Set up large pieces of paper outside and let your kids make their own masterpieces by blowing bubbles onto the paper.

92

Pair off into teams of two. Draw a letter, word, or picture on your teammate's back using your finger and have them guess what you've drawn by drawing it on a piece of paper.

93

Make owls out of brown paper lunch bags by drawing faces on the bottom of the bags and adding feathers or using markers to add any colors you'd like.

Give yourselves avocado facials.

Ingredients
1 ripe avocado, cut in half and pitted
1 tablespoon honey

Directions
- Scoop out the avocado and mash in a bowl until creamy.
- Add the honey and mix until the mixture forms a uniform paste.
- Apply the mixture to your face and leave on for 10 to 15 minutes, then rinse off with lukewarm water and pat dry.

Learn how to speak Pig Latin.

- If the word you want to say begins with a consonant or consonant cluster (like "hello" or "switch"), move the consonants to the end of the word and add "-ay" to the end. For example, "hello" becomes "ello-hay" and "switch" becomes "itch-sway."

- If the word you want to say begins with a vowel (like "apple"), simply add "-yay," "-way," or "-ay" to the end of the word, depending on your preference. So "apple" would become "apple-yay."

- If the word you want to say begins with a "Y" (like "yellow" or "my"), treat it like you would a consonant. However, if the "Y" comes at the end of a consonant cluster (like in "rhythm"), it is treated like a vowel and does not move to the end of the word.

- Remember to split up compound words (like "bedroom" or "sauce-pan") to make it even harder for non-Pig Latin speakers to know what you're saying!

hello ⟶ ello-hay

96

Have a library scavenger hunt. Many libraries have their own scavenger hunts already set up, or you can make a list of your kids' favorite books and have them ask a librarian to help them use the Dewey decimal system.

97

If you have older children, play paint ball.

98

Make your own fairy garden out of recycled materials, complete with doors, roads, and painted rocks.

99

Pick strawberries at a local farm.

100

Make a video of your kids interviewing you about your life, then switch and interview them. Have an annual family movie night where you watch the interviews from years past.

101

Play shadow tag. Shadow tag is just like normal tag, except you have to "tag" the person's shadow by stepping on it in order for them to become "it."

102

Have a weed pulling contest in your garden. Whoever cleans out the most weeds gets to decide one plant you should grow next season.

103

Watch the cake makers at a big box store decorate the cakes and cookies.

104

Play exquisite corpse. Each person writes down the first sentence of a story and then passes it to the person to their right, folding the paper so the last sentence is covered. The next person then writes whatever sentence they want, covering it as well before it goes to the next person. At the end, read your stories out loud to see what you came up with.

105

Paint outdoors using washable paints and recycled cardboard.

106

Have an epic Harry Potter wand fight, complete with your own sound effects.

107

Make a bottle tornado complete with glitter. Take two 2-liter bottles and fill them both halfway with water. Add glitter to each bottle, then connect them in the middle using either Duct Tape or a specially made screw-on cap. Once connected, swirl the bottom and top bottle until you make your very own miniature tornado.

108

Have a thumb war.

IT DIDN'T MATTER

HOUSE WAS; IT

THERE WAS

HOW BIG OUR MATTERED THAT LOVE IN IT.

—Peter Buffett

109

Draw a picture blindfolded. Have the rest of your family silently guess what you drew and draw their own version of it without a blindfold. Once they all draw their answers, tell them what you drew and see what everyone came up with!

110

Make a volcano outside in the snow. Following the directions to make a regular soda bottle volcano (see page 202), create a mountain of snow with a hole in the center. Place the bottle of vinegar mixture into the center of the volcano, quickly pour in the baking soda, and step back!

111

Make a classic handprint turkey.

112

Make a time capsule. You can include drawings, pictures, letters to your future selves, or anything else you want. Then, bury the time capsule or hide it away in your house and open it as soon (or as late) as you want.

113

Go on an indoor stuffed animal safari.

114

Teach your kids "old school" games like red rover.

115
Go snorkeling.

116
Create colorful salt paintings. All you need is card stock, glue, salt, and liquid water-colors. First, let your kids trace out a design on the card stock using glue. Next, cover the glue in salt and gently shake off the extra. Then, using the liquid watercolors and a paint brush, add color to the drawing. The paint will travel along the salt and make incredible pictures. Keep in mind this project may take up to 2 days to dry.

117
Celebrate half birthdays.

118
Label all the things in your house with a new language you want to learn.

119
Host an arts and crafts party.

120
Visit the library and have each kid pick out a time in history. Then, find one kids' book each on that subject and read them as a family.

121
Play Quiddler.

122
Make holiday cards for hospital patients.

Make the coolest catapult ever.

Tools

2 small Popsicle sticks
2 large tongue depressors
4 rubber bands
Small objects, to launch

Directions

- Lay down a small Popsicle stick. Place 1 tongue depressor in the center of the small Popsicle stick, allowing about 1½ inches of the larger stick to rest over one side.

- Lay the second smaller Popsicle stick on top and rubber band both ends tightly so the tongue depressor is pressed between the two smaller ones.

- Place the second tongue depressor on top of the first one and rubber band the two short ends together about ½ inch from the tip. Using the last rubber band, crisscross the center of the two tongue depressors so the rubber band wraps around the base of the catapult and the top.

- To use your catapult, place a small object on the top long end of the larger stick. Press down on the front short end of the stick and the longer end at the same time. Release the longer end and allow the small object to soar.

Make popcorn balls.

Ingredients

7 quarts popped popcorn
1 cup granulated sugar
1 cup light corn syrup
¼ cup water
¼ teaspoon salt
3 tablespoons unsalted butter
1 teaspoon vanilla extract

Directions

- Heat the oven to 200°F. Place the popcorn on a large baking sheet and place in the oven to keep warm.

- In a heavy-bottomed saucepan, add the sugar, corn syrup, water, and salt. Cook over medium heat until the mixture is 235°F.

- Remove from heat, add the butter and vanilla, and stir until the butter is melted. Remove the popcorn from the oven and pour the mixture over the popcorn, stirring until evenly coated.

- Once cool enough to handle, shape the popcorn into palm-sized balls, using cold water to keep your hands from sticking to the candy. Allow to cool until hardened.

125

Make a mobile together using found objects, dowels, and string. You can also include family pictures, if you'd like.

126

Lie in a hammock together and read a book aloud.

127

Write a poem together.

128

Make a secret code. You can create your own decoder ring or swap out letters for numbers. Just be sure to make a key in case you forget the code!

129

Learn the rhythm to the "Cups" song and do the motions to your favorite songs.

130

Make boats out of recyclables and go float them at the pond. Be sure to clean up after yourselves!

131

Play Chutes and Ladders.

132

Learn about Indigenous Peoples' Day and why it's important that we learn about indigenous cultures, their histories, and to respect their traditions.

133

Build a birdhouse. You can either pick up a birdhouse kit at your local lumber shop or make your own using Popsicle sticks and a hot glue gun.

134

Volunteer to walk dogs at your local shelter.

135

Visit a national park. Many national parks are free to visit and have a wide range of family-friendly activities year-round.

136

Take a dip in a small pool filled with water balloons.

137

Go to a ballgame and teach your kids (and yourself) how to keep a scorecard.

138

Take a weekend road trip.

139

Participate in a flash mob.

140

Play kick the can.

141

Go geo-caching or letterboxing.

142

Play Trivial Pursuit.

Make papier-mâché hot air balloon models.

Tools
- 3 parts white glue
- 1 part water
- 2 tablespoons salt
- Newspaper strips
- Balloons
- Small baskets
- String
- Paint

Directions
- Mix glue, water, and salt together thoroughly. If you live in a humid location, use less water. If you live in a dry location, use more water. Keep in mind that more than 4 layers of papier-mâché will not dry correctly.

- Blow up the balloons, cover in papier-mâché-dipped strips of newspaper, and allow to dry. Once dry, pop the balloons, attach the basket to the bottom of the balloon with string, and paint as desired.

Make homemade eggnog during the holidays.

Ingredients
½ teaspoon vanilla extract
¾ teaspoon nutmeg, grated, plus more for topping
1 cup granulated sugar, plus 1 tablespoon
2 cups heavy cream
2 cups milk
6 eggs, beaten until frothy (you can get cartons of pasteurized eggs at the grocery store)

Directions
- Whisk the vanilla, nutmeg, sugar, cream, and milk into the beaten eggs. When thoroughly combined, chill in the refrigerator until ready to serve. Pour into glasses and garnish with the additional nutmeg.

145
Make a campfire.

146
Make a fort with driftwood
and sticks found on the beach.

147
Have a funky hairdo day.
Let your kids play around with
temporary hair color, braids,
spikes, gel, and more!

148
Go fly a kite and learn about
wind science.

149
Teach your kids how
to jump rope.

150
Play tag with
the whole family.

151
Collect beach glass
and make a mosaic using hot
glue and paper plates
or cardboard.

152
Let your kids "decorate"
plates for a special family
dinner using condiments like
ketchup, barbeque sauce,
and mustard.

153
Perfect your handstands
and cartwheels.

154
Set up a bucket and rope pulley contraption to deliver things from one floor of your house to the other.

155
Play pin the nose on the pumpkin.

156
Learn about St. Lucia Day and talk about how light and community are important things to celebrate when it's cold and dark outside during the winter.

157
Have a paper boat engineering contest.

158
Make a target with chalk on a blackboard or the sidewalk, and then throw wet sponges at it until it disappears.

159
Make a marshmallow catapult using a spoon and see who can catch the most in their mouth.

160
Create your own indoor "drive-in" movie theater with cardboard cars.

161
Teach your kids how to use a pogo stick.

FAMILIES ARE MOSTLY SWEET

LIKE FUDGE—
WITH A FEW NUTS.

—Unknown

162
Have a fall leaf scavenger hunt and see who can find the biggest or reddest leaves.

163
Make marshmallow constellations using licorice to connect the dots.

164
Learn about St. Patrick's Day and why it's important for people to remember where they came from and celebrate their cultures. Make sure you wear green while you celebrate—it's tradition!

165
Take turns reading a story together using funny voices.

166
Have a monthly wacky meal where everyone chooses one dish to make. It's okay if they are foods that don't go together at all, like pancakes and meatloaf.

167
Learn how to make friendship bracelets.

168
Make a rain gauge using a tall tube or vase marked in measurement increments. Set it in an open area that will get plenty of rain. Have your kids track the next rainstorm and see how much water you get.

169
Make a scarecrow.

170
Finger-paint on your windows with washable bathtub paints.

171
Do blind taste tests with various drinks and food and see who can guess the most foods.

172
Make spider decorations using black construction paper and googly eyes, then hang them all over the house for a spooky surprise.

173
Go snowboarding.

174
Create calming glitter jars by mixing glitter in water and adding it to a mason jar. To avoid messes, glue the lid shut with a hot glue gun.

175
Set up a pretend coffee shop in the living room.

176
Go on a long-distance family road trip.

177
Make bows and arrows from found objects.

178
Create instruments out of stuff you find in the park and then have a jam session.

Bake a jumbo cookie and eat it like a pie.

Ingredients

2 sticks unsalted butter, at room temperature
½ cup granulated sugar
1 cup brown sugar
2 eggs
2 teaspoons vanilla extract
1 teaspoon baking soda
2 teaspoons hot water
½ teaspoon salt
2½ cups flour
2 cups semi-sweet chocolate chips

Directions

· Preheat the oven to 375°F. Heat a 12-inch cast-iron skillet in the oven while making the batter.

· In a large bowl, beat the butter and sugars together until light and fluffy. Add the eggs one at a time, being sure to combine thoroughly before proceeding. Stir in the vanilla.

· Dissolve the baking soda in the hot water and add to the batter with the salt. Stir in the flour and chocolate chips.

- Remove the skillet from the oven and put the batter in it, smoothing the top with a spatula.
- Put the skillet in the oven and cook until golden brown, about 15 minutes.

180

Learn string games like cat's cradle.

181

Make slingshots.

182

Try fly swatter painting using fly swatters as your brushes. Make sure to do this outside as there can be some splatter.

183

Skip rocks at the lake.

184

Visit a farmers market and try a new fruit or vegetable.

185

Play Trouble.

186

Go snow shoeing.

187

Have a coin-flip road trip. Starting from your home, drive until you reach an intersection, then flip a coin. On "heads" go right, and on "tails" go left. Do this for each subsequent intersection. The trip ends when you've reached a fun destination.

188

Play Candyland.

189

Raise chickens or goats as pets.

190

Attend an opera.

191
Do anything that involves bubble wrap.

192
Have an impressions contest.

193
Plant a tree that you will take an annual family picture in front of.

194
Paint with pasta. All you need is uncooked pasta in all kinds of fun shapes, washable paint, and paper or card stock. Dip the pasta in the paint and use the shapes to make prints or faces!

195
Host a tea party.

196
Play an item memory game. Get together a bunch of random objects from all over the house. Cover them with a towel or blanket and set a timer for 30 seconds. Pull back the blanket and let your kids stare at the items for 30 seconds, then cover them back up and have them write down as many as they can remember. See who can remember the most objects.

197
Go for a walk in the rain together.

198
Host your own family "drive-in" slide show in the back yard.

199

Invest in an ice cream maker to make your own homemade ice cream.

Ingredients

3 cups heavy cream
1 cup whole milk
¾ cup granulated sugar
1 teaspoon salt
Yolks of 5 large eggs, beaten
Seeds of 2 vanilla beans

Directions

- In a medium saucepan, warm the cream, milk, sugar, and salt over medium heat. Stir until the sugar has dissolved.

- While whisking constantly, add 1 cup of the warm milk mixture to the bowl containing the egg yolks. Add the tempered eggs to the saucepan and cook over medium heat until the mixture thickens enough to coat the back of a wooden spoon.

- Add the vanilla seeds and remove the pan from heat. Strain into a bowl through a fine sieve and stir the mixture as it cools.

- When the mixture has cooled completely, cover with plastic wrap and place in the refrigerator for 6 hours.

- Remove the mixture from the refrigerator and pour it into an ice cream maker. Churn until the desired texture is achieved. Place the churned cream in the freezer for 6 hours before serving.

200
Go for a walk during the full moon.

201
Create a "pay it forward" line at a local fast food chain or store by paying for the person behind you in line.

202
Play limbo.

203
Create your own family history by choosing one of your distant relatives and making up a story. Each person adds a line to the story as you go around. See how silly you can be.

204
Hunt for a four-leafed clover.

205
Plant a succulent garden.

206
Learn about Passover (also called Pesach) and discuss the importance of sharing stories of the past, as well as preserving cultural traditions across generations.

207
Collect acorns and paint faces on them.

208
Play backgammon.

209
Watch birds build a nest
(or maybe even see them
feed the baby birds).

210
Go window shopping.

211
Make shell necklaces after
a beach trip. Make sure to boil
the shells first to help
reduce any smell.

212
Play a round of horseshoes.

213
Go ziplining.

214
Have a water bucket relay.

215
Watch the sunset.

216
Make a giant connect-the-dots
picture in your backyard using
disks of cardboard as the
"dots" and connecting
them with string.

217
Make outdoor game board on
your deck. You can make it as
big or small as you want and
use whatever you find around
the house as part of the game.

218
Play charades.

219
Press leaves into a
photo album.

CALL IT A CLAN, NETWORK, CALL CALL IT A FAMILY; CALL IT, ARE, YOU

CALL IT A
IT A TRIBE,
WHATEVER YOU
WHOEVER YOU
NEED ONE.

—Jane Howard

220

Play gotcha.

How to play:

- One player will be the moderator who keeps track of points and keeps an eye on the rules.

- First, establish what each person can use to "get" another person. This can be spray bottles, foam pool noodles, or even balloons. The goal is to make sure no one gets hurt. The object of the game is to "get" other players using your "getter" of choice, without getting "gotten" yourself.

- You've been "gotten" if someone taps you with their "getter." Whoever is left standing wins!

Make soap clouds.

Tools
- 1 Ivory soap bar
- 1 microwavable plate

Directions
- Place the unwrapped soap on the plate, put in the microwave, and heat on high for 1 to 2 minutes, until the soap has stopped expanding and you have a soap cloud left behind. Keep in mind this only works with Ivory soap.

222

Build sandcastles.

223

Get involved in local "help the environment" days.

224

Make your own pop-up book by taking a small notebook and drawing a picture on a separate piece of paper. Cut this picture out and fold it down the middle. Take two different pieces of paper and glue them to each page individually, making sure they meet the edges of the drawing but not all the way to the center. Glue the pieces of paper to the picture, close the book, and then open it to see your new pop-up book.

225

Go horseback riding.

226

Learn sign language.

227

Go paper plate skating on linoleum by standing on paper plates and "skating" around the area. You can also try getting a running start and see how far you can "skate."

228

Play hide-and-seek.

229

Go on a cruise.

230

Have a rainbow dinner using foods of all different colors.

231

Build a backyard ice skating rink.

232

Create a new voicemail message together.

233

Play homemade Jeopardy. You can print out your own questions or write them on index cards, and have each kid make a buzzing noise before they answer a question. Be sure to include topics your kids have been learning in school for educational fun.

234

Watch geese flying south for the winter.

235

Don't let the handprint turkey feel left out! Create different kinds of animals from handprints and display them.

236

Using white shelf paper or the inside of brown grocery bags, design your own wrapping paper with crayons, magic markers, or paints. Then, use them to wrap a present for a friend or family member.

237

Have a puzzle race. Use puzzles with the same number of pieces and see who finishes first. Be sure to display the results.

Make your own snow globes.

Tools
Superglue or a hot glue gun
Plastic figurine
Small glass jar with a lid
Water
Glitter
Sequins
Glycerin (optional)

Directions
- Glue your figurine of choice to the lid of the glass jar.

- Fill the jar with cold water, then add the glitter and sequins and stir. Add a few drops the glycerin, if using.

- Screw on the lid. For added security, glue the lid into place.

- Flip the jar over and shake to see the "snow" fall.

Make berry jam.

Ingredients

6 cups strawberries, hulled, cored, and quartered
2 cups blueberries
2 cups raspberries
½ cup sugar
1¼ tablespoons pectin

Directions

- Place the berries and sugar in a large saucepan and cook, while stirring, over medium-high heat. When the sugar has dissolved and the berries start breaking down and releasing their liquid, reduce the heat to medium and cook, while stirring every 10 minutes, until the berries are very soft and the mixture has thickened, about 30 to 40 minutes.

- While stirring the jam, sprinkle the pectin onto the mixture and cook for another minute until the berries are soft.

- Transfer the jam to mason jars and store in the refrigerator for up to 1 week or freeze for longer.

240

Have a pool noodle fight.

241

Learn about Día de los Muertos and discuss why it's important to remember those who are no longer with us and to celebrate family togetherness.

242

Go rock climbing or bouldering.

243

Paint in the snow using squirt bottles, water, and food coloring. Remember: a little food coloring goes a long way.

244

Play ladder golf.

245

Add glitter to white playdough to make snow playdough.

246

Have a no rules night (within reason). Let your kids have dessert before the meal, have a dance party at bedtime, or even go for a late-night walk around the backyard.

247

Build an ice castle by filling different containers with water and then freezing them. Then, stack the objects together to make an ice castle. If you're having trouble getting your building blocks to stick together, try adding a bit of salt to help melt the ice.

248

Play Jenga.

249

Start a family blog.
Take turns updating it from
different perspectives.

250

Play human knot.
Get everyone together in
a circle, and have them join
hands with two people across
the middle of the circle. Once
everyone has linked hands,
the goal is to untangle the
human knot without letting
go of anyone's hands. This
requires real teamwork, so be
sure to take your time and help
younger players. Once you're
all standing in a circle with
your hands untangled,
you've won!

251

Go to a flea market.

252

Make a family music video.

253

Make squirrels out of
toilet paper tubes. Simply
paint squirrel faces onto
toilet paper tubes and then
make tails and ears out of
construction paper to glue on
the sides. You can even add
real acorns if you want.

254

Play a round of mini golf.

255

Pretend to be pirates for a day
by dressing up in costumes,
planning a treasure hunt,
and talking like a pirate.

256

Bake cookies for
a local fundraiser.

Ingredients:

1 stick unsalted butter
1¼ cup flour
½ teaspoon baking soda
½ teaspoon salt
½ cup packed light brown sugar
¼ cup granulated sugar
1 egg
1 teaspoon vanilla extract
1 cup semi-sweet chocolate chips

Directions

- Preheat oven to 375°F. While the oven preheats, soften the butter by placing it in the microwave for 7-second increments, turning the butter each time until it is soft to the touch and nearly melting.

- Line a cookie sheet with parchment paper. In a medium bowl, whisk together the flour, baking soda, and salt.

- In a large bowl, combine the butter and sugars and beat on medium speed until light and fluffy. Beat in the egg and vanilla.

- Gradually stir in the flour mixture until well blended, then stir the chocolate chips into the cookie dough.

- Place the dough in spoonfuls onto the cookie sheet. Bake for 12 to 15 minutes until lightly browned. Transfer the cookies to wire racks to cool as you continue to make batches.

257
Make paper snowflakes.

258
Carve shapes into bars of soap using dental floss and toothpicks.

259
Spin until you're dizzy and then do a 50-yard dash.

260
Play a game of badminton.

261
Have multiplication table races.

262
"Adopt" a wild animal through your favorite wildlife foundation.

263
Sail leaf boats down a creek together and see whose boat is fastest.

264
Host an outdoor movie night.

265
Volunteer at an elder care organization.

266
Look for animal tracks in nature.

267
Have your kids create a summer-fun scrapbook by keeping a journal about their favorite summer activities and adding pictures and drawings to help them remember the season!

268
Go sledding.

269
Have a "blind date" with a book by wrapping your favorite books in paper and then randomly choosing one to read out loud.

270
Make your own pet rock.

271
Create pinecone birds using craft feathers, googly eyes, and a hot glue gun.

272
Play pond (or rink) hockey.

273
Go tubing on the water.

274
Have a snowball fight with pom-poms.

275
Create a lawn maze.

276
Make mazes or puzzles for each other to solve.

277
Get fun paper and an origami book or look up origami videos online. Learn how to create your favorite animals together and use them to decorate the house.

278
Visit a local museum.

279
Play ring toss.

FAMILY AND

HIDDEN

SEEK THEM

THEIR

FRIENDS ARE TREASURES, AND ENJOY RICHES.

—Wanda Hope Carter

280

Go stargazing.

281

Make melted pony bead crafts. You can find pony bead kits at most craft stores. Just make sure to put parchment paper or a washcloth between your iron and the beads when you set them, otherwise you may be in for a melted mess!

282

Build a rocket ship out of cardboard.

283

Learn about Boxing Day and the tradition of giving presents to families who are less fortunate.

284

Play the license plate game on a road trip. This works best on long road trips. The goal is to call out a license plate that isn't from the state you are in currently, but also hasn't been called out before. If you're going on a shorter trip, you can always call out license plates starting with each letter of the alphabet in order.

285

Build a snow fort.

286

Make a "pet" jellyfish in a jar by adding a plastic jellyfish to a mason jar full of water. You can add glitter and food coloring, if you'd like, just be sure to glue the lid shut.

287

Visit an airport and watch the planes take off and land.

288

Play tug-of-war as a family, being sure to balance the ages and strengths on both teams for maximum fun.

289

Make homemade holiday cards.

290

Have a "beach day" in your living room, complete with an umbrella, beach towels, and "water" in the form of a blue blanket. You can even dress up in your bathing suits and watch summer movies.

291

Go for a hike.

292

Create pressed flower window gardens by picking your favorite outdoor flowers and pressing them between waxed paper. Be sure to stack heavy books or weights on top to get them as thin as possible. Once dried, hang them in your windows to create your own year-round garden.

293

Decorate a pair of jeans together using fabric paint, then have a fashion show.

294

Play Marco Polo at the pool.

Make homemade gak.

Ingredients

½ cup water
1 cup cornstarch
Food coloring (optional)

Directions

- Combine the water and cornstarch in a bowl. Mix until smooth, then add the food coloring and stir. Store in an airtight container when not in use.

Play the gift wrap game.

Tools
    1 main present
    Lots of gift wrap
    Tape
    Small gifts like candy, toys, or plastic rings

How to play:

- Wrap the main present with as many layers of wrapping paper as you want.

- Once the present has been wrapped, have each player go in a circle and unwrap one layer of wrapping paper. Then, they pass it to the next person. Play music in the background while people unwrap the gift and pause it randomly.

- Whoever is holding the gift when the song is paused gets a smaller gift, and the person to unwrap the final layer of wrapping paper gets the main present.

297

Build a snowman.

298

Play backyard Yahtzee with giant dice and a bucket.

299

Have a show-and-tell day.

300

Do a random act of kindness.

301

Have a home photo shoot where your kids act as the photographers. Let them costume direct the photos and set up their own backgrounds.

302

Design a house and tell others about it.

303

Have a white elephant gift swap.

304

Go cross-country skiing.

305

Have a "favorite color" dinner using foods that are all the same color.

306

Go on a creek walk.

307

Play the related words game. Going in a circle, have one person come up with a word. The next person has 3 seconds to come up with a related word before they are out. Remember, no repeats!

308

Play freeze tag.

309

Make tin can stilts using large tin cans and two strings. This project requires you to drill two holes in each can to thread the strings through, but the result is well worth the added effort.

310

Assign secret Santas to each other for a week when it's not the holidays.

311

Go ice skating.

312

Have a sing-along together in the car.

313

Visit a batting cage.

314

Have a pet talent contest.

315

Go for a ski-do ride.

316

Learn to say "thank you" in another language. Here are some to get you started!
French: *Merci* (mer-sea)
Spanish: *Gracias* (gra-sea-as)
German: *Danke* (dan-ke) or the more formal *dankeschön* (dan-ke shern)

317

Have breakfast in bed. Take turns being the server and the served.

Make homemade pizzas.

Ingredients
¾ cup warm water (110 to 115°F)
1 teaspoon active dry yeast
2 cups all-purpose flour, plus more for dusting
1½ teaspoons salt
Toppings of choice
1 tablespoon olive oil

Directions
- Preheat the oven to 450°F.

- In a large bowl, add the warm water and yeast, stirring to dissolve the yeast. Stir in the flour and salt and mix until the dough is just combined. It will be sticky.

- Turn out on a floured surface and start kneading until the flour is incorporated, adding more if necessary to make the dough malleable and smooth, but not overdone.

- Allow the dough to rest for 15 minutes. While it's doing so, put a 12-inch cast-iron skillet in the oven. Prepare the toppings for the pizza.

- After 15 minutes or when ready, put a piece of parchment paper under the dough. Start rolling and pushing it out to form a 9-inch disk that will fit in the skillet. If it bounces back, let it rest before pushing or rolling it out again.

- When the disk is formed, use potholders or oven mitts to remove the skillet from the oven. Add the olive oil and brush to distribute over the bottom. Transfer the dough to the skillet and add the toppings.

- Bake for 12 to 15 minutes until the crust starts to brown and the toppings are hot and bubbling. Remove from the oven.

- Allow to cool for 5 minutes before lifting or sliding the pizza out and serving.

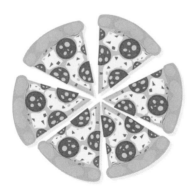

319
Tee up at a driving range.

320
Have an ugly sweater contest.

321
Buy electronics at a yard sale and then take them apart.

322
Play red light, green light.

323
Create a sun dial using a circular piece of paper and a stick and use it to teach your kids about telling time. Make sure to mark the time on the piece of paper as the sun moves throughout the day, then see how the marks line up in a week or a month later.

324
Harvest pumpkins.

325
Once you get the hang of making your favorite origami creations, make a dozen of them and string them together into a garland.

326
Learn an instrument together.

327
Create a wallet out of Duct Tape by folding a piece of paper in half, taping the short ends, and then covering everything but the top opening slit in Duct Tape.

328
Play Mad Libs.

329
Make shadow puppets.

330
Race to see who can complete their chores the fastest. The winner gets to pick what's for dinner.

331
Make something together and then sell it.

332
Get succulents and cacti and make decorations for them out of construction paper. You can make glasses, little hats, or even superhero capes!

333
Go for a hike in the snow.

334
Work on a crossword puzzle together.

335
Have a hula hooping contest to see who can spin their hoops the longest or who can keep the most hoops going at once.

336
Take a dance class.

337
Go to a minor-league baseball game.

338
Make a nature collage.

339
Play Mouse Trap.

ONLY WHERE IS THERE CHANCE

CHILDREN GATHER ANY REAL OF FUN.

—Mignon McLaughlin

340
Catch butterflies
(and release them).

341
Play in the sprinklers.

342
Create a thankfulness
tree for your dining room
by making the leaves out of
handprints. You can then write
something you are thankful for
on every leaf and share them
together at dinner.

343
Have an arts and crafts day.

344
Fill water balloons with
small toys and water, then pop
them for a fun surprise!

345
Have a soccer shoot out.

346
Go on a spooky
graveyard tour.

347
Play Family Feud.

348
Play messy Twister using
flour or washable body
paint on each spot.

349
Plan a backyard dinner.

350
Have an outdoor painting
party using huge canvases
or cardboard.

351
Learn how to do yo-yo tricks.

352
Attend a play.

353
Play Boggle.

354
Host silly relay races. Set the course up and then have your kids hop on one foot, run backward, skip, or even walk like a crab! The sillier the race the better.

355
Learn magic tricks.

356
Play Kerplunk.

357
Go ice block sledding on grass with a towel-covered block of ice. If you have a large enough freezer, you can even fill a small storage bin with water and use the resulting flat piece of ice as a more comfortable sled.

358
Host a BBQ.

359
Cover a slide with shaving cream and slide down (wearing bathing suits for easy clean up, of course).

360
Go sock skating through your house. Just be careful around sharp corners!

Make marshmallows.

Ingredients

1 cup water
3 packets gelatin
1½ cups granulated sugar
1 cup light corn syrup
Seeds of 2 vanilla beans
Confectioners' sugar, for dusting

Directions

- Place ½ cup of the water in the bowl of a stand mixer. Sprinkle the gelatin into the water and let the gelatin dissolve.

- Place the remaining water, sugar, and corn syrup in a saucepan and cook, while swirling the pan occasionally, over medium heat until the mixture is 240°F. Remove the pan from heat and let stand for 1 minute.

- Fit the stand mixer with the whisk attachment and run it at low speed while slowly pouring the contents of the saucepan down the side of the mixing bowl.

- Gradually increase the speed of the mixer until the mixture is white, fluffy, and glossy. Add the vanilla seeds and whisk to incorporate.

- Sift the confectioners' sugar over a greased 9 x 13-inch baking dish until the dish is completely coated. Pour the mixture into the baking dish and use a greased rubber spatula to even out the surface. Let stand for 6 hours.

- When ready to serve, dust a work surface, a knife, and your hands with confectioners' sugar. Transfer the block of marshmallow to the work surface, cut into cubes, and serve.

362

Make fall wreaths using leaves, sticks, or anything else that comes to mind.

363

Visit a historic house or farm and find out how people used to live in the past.

364

Have a hot chocolate bar night complete with marshmallows, candies, whipped cream, and, of course, sprinkles.

365

Visit a nature center.

366

Turn your family room into a spa complete with cucumber slices and relaxing music.

367

Make your own super smoothie with all the fruits and vegetables you can imagine.

368

Help your neighbor shovel their driveway.

369

Swim in a public pool.

370

Find an easy-to-assemble shelf or piece of furniture and put it together as a family.

371

Make beaded bracelets, necklaces, or other decorations together.

372

Jump waves in the sea.

373

Learn about Diwali and the importance of celebrating life and light as a community, as well as how the start of a new year is observed on different days in different cultures.

374

Play Scrabble.

375

Host a Halloween party.

376

Play with clay, then bake your creations to make them permanent.

377

Have a completely candlelit dinner together. No electric lights allowed!

378

Make invisible ink and send secret messages to each other. You can use white crayons on normal printer paper and then color over it with markers to reveal the message, or if you want to be even more crafty you can mix lemon juice with a few drops of water, write on the page, allow to dry, and then reveal the message by holding it over a lightbulb or (carefully) over a candle.

379

Make a box town out of old boxes.

Play naughty or nice during the holidays.

How to play:

- Each player goes around the circle and asks another player to pick between "naughty" or "nice." If they choose "nice," the player gets to ask them a question of their choice, though they should try and stay on a holiday theme.

- If they refuse to answer the question or choose "naughty," the player can choose to have them do something ridiculous, like wear a candy cane on their head for the rest of the night or sing a Christmas carol on video. If they refuse, they're out of the game. The game ends when there is only one player left in the circle.

Make borax crystal snowflakes.

Tools

3 (5-inch) pipe cleaners, plus 6 (1½-inch) pipe cleaners
Pencil
String
Mason jar
3 tablespoons borax
Blue food coloring (optional)
1 cup boiling water

Directions

- Twist the three 5-inch pieces of pipe cleaner together to form a snowflake shape with six points. Then, add the smaller pipe cleaners to the end of each point and bend into a triangle shape to complete the snowflake frame.

- Tie the snowflake to the pencil using a piece of string, leaving enough slack that the snowflake does not touch the bottom of the jar, but can be covered with liquid.

- Combine the borax, 1 drop of food coloring, if using, and the boiling water. Pour the mixture into the jar and allow to sit overnight. Remove, dry, and display.

382

Have a water gun race. Punch a hole through the bottom of two or more plastic cups and thread yarn through the holes. Hang the cups up across the same area, separated enough so they do not touch. Using a squirt gun or water sprayer, shoot water into the cup to race it down the string. Whoever reaches the end of the string first wins!

383

Go to a lake and watch boats.

384

Make family silhouettes. Using a projector or bright flashlight, have someone sit in front of a blank piece of paper. Trace their silhouette, then remove and fill in however you want.

385

Plan "Mystery Thursdays" with surprise activities.

386

Make balloon yo-yos using inflated balloons and long rubber bands. Simply tie the rubber band to the end of balloon and have fun!

387

Make a candy corn wreath using a circular piece of cardboard, candy corn, and glue. Make sure to hang it on your front door to get in the festive spirit.

388

Let the kids cook dinner (with supervision for younger kids, of course).

Play chain tag. Whoever gets tagged has to join hands with whoever is "it" and try and catch other players. The game ends when everyone is part of the chain.

Make sun catchers. Simply collect sea glass or pick up colored gems from the store. Take an unmatched container lid and arrange the colorful pieces on the lid, then cover up to the rim of the lid with clear glue. Allow to dry, then hang on the nearest window and enjoy!

Play pumpkin toss and see how far you can throw each pumpkin!

Visit a Renaissance faire.

Start a round story where each person adds a word using the first line: *There was a monster who wasn't mean, not even a little bit...*

Construct a mini water wheel by taking a disposable plastic plate and gluing small plastic cups around the edge on their side, with the openings all facing the same direction. Place a skewer through the center of the plate and hold under running water to watch the wheel spin.

Go fishing.

YOUR CHILDREN
IMPOSSIBLE TO
THEY'RE ITS

MAKE IT REGRET YOUR PAST. FINEST FRUITS.

—Anna Quindlen

396
Send a message in a bottle.

397
Learn about Kwanzaa and how holidays can help bring people from different parts of the world together to celebrate their heritage.

398
Take a drive in the country.

399
Dress each other up as toilet paper mummies.

400
Go head-to-head and see who can make the wildest cookies while blindfolded. Make sure to lay down a tablecloth, this can get messy!

401
Play The Game of Life.

402
Have a hands-free marshmallow eating contest. Whoever can get the most marshmallows into their mouth without using their hands wins.

403
Learn the alphabet backward.

404
Measure everyone's height on a door frame.

405
Write and illustrate a short story about an imaginary animal.

406
Make a Diet Coke and Mentos eruption.

407
Go to a rock-climbing wall.

408
Send postcards to family and friends.

409
Take a photo once a week for a year. At the end of the year, combine all the photos into a scrapbook. You can even take a picture in the same area of your backyard to see how things change throughout the seasons.

410
Go on a bus or trolley ride.

411
Play soccer.

412
Start a family book club.

413
Play school at home, with the kids teaching the parents. Make sure you don't forget recess!

414
Have a family talent show.

415
Play Yahtzee.

416
Visit a recycling plant and learn how to reduce, reuse, and recycle.

Play deck the halls.

Tools
Plastic ornaments
Tinsel
Decorative strings
Any other holiday decorations

How to play:
- In this game, one player gets to be the Christmas tree of their dreams. Splitting up into teams of two or more, each team's goal is to decorate their "Christmas tree" the fastest using all the decorations provided. The player being decorated cannot help in any way at all, other than verbal instructions. Whoever completes their Christmas tree first, wins!

Make mug cakes and decorate them.

Ingredients

¼ cup all-purpose flour
¼ cup granulated sugar
2 tablespoons unsweetened cocoa powder
⅛ teaspoon baking soda
⅛ teaspoon salt
3 tablespoons milk
2 tablespoons canola oil
1 tablespoon water
¼ teaspoon vanilla extract
Chocolate chips (optional), to taste

Directions

- Mix the flour, sugar, cocoa powder, baking soda, and salt in a large, microwave-safe mug. Add the milk, canola oil, water, and vanilla extract and stir well. If desired, add the chocolate chips and stir.

- Cook in the microwave for about 1 minute 45 seconds, or until the cake is done in the middle. The cook time can vary depending on the type of microwave.

417

Pretend to be werewolves together and howl at the full moon.

420

Play kickball.

421

Learn how to read a map and go on an adventure together.

422

Have a finger-painting day.

423

Learn about Yule and the celebration of the Winter Solstice and talk about how people have been finding ways to bring brightness to the darkest day of the year for thousands of years.

424

Play outdoor tic-tac-toe using balls and pool noodles.

425

Make homemade pasta as a family.

426

Make animated flipbooks out of sticky notes by starting a drawing at one corner of the pad of notes, and then having it move on each subsequent pad. Flip the edge of the pad to see your figure in action!

427

Hold an international food sampling night.

428

Climb a tree.

429
Read a book, then watch the movie.

430
Using a globe or map, randomly pick a continent or country, then make a food from that area.

431
Play Codenames.

432
Enroll in a summer reading program.

433
Build an awesome pillow fort.

434
Blow on a blade of grass and make it whistle.

435
Visit an aquarium.

436
Play flashlight tag.

437
Have a sumo-style wrestling match using pillows, blankets, and oversized coats as padding.

438
Play with soap foam.

439
Make your own piñata using papier-mâché and balloons. Just be sure to leave an opening to add candy!

440
Write a soldier a letter.

Play heads up 7 up.

How to play:

- Have all but one person sit down with their heads down, their eyes closed, and their thumbs up. The one person left standing quietly chooses one person to be "it" while everyone else keeps their eyes closed.

- The person who is "it" chooses up to three people, then sits back down and puts their head down with their eyes closed.

- The person left standing says, "Heads up!" and the people who had their thumbs pressed down stand up. They then try and guess who tagged their thumbs. Whoever guesses correctly first then gets to be the one to choose who is "it" next round.

Make muddy buddies.

Ingredients
- 1 cup semi-sweet chocolate chips
- ¾ cup creamy peanut butter
- 1 teaspoon pure vanilla extract
- 9 cups square rice cereal
- 1½ cups confectioners' sugar

Directions
- Place the chocolate chips and peanut butter in a microwave-safe bowl and microwave for 30 seconds. Remove from the microwave, add the vanilla, and stir until the mixture is smooth.

- Place the rice cereal in a large bowl and pour the chocolate-peanut butter mixture over the cereal. Carefully mix until the pieces are coated.

- Place the cereal into a large plastic bag and add confectioners' sugar. Seal the bag and shake until each piece is coated with sugar.

- Line a baking sheet with parchment paper and pour the cereal onto the baking sheet. Place the sheet in the refrigerator and chill for 30 to 45 minutes.

443
Go caroling for charity.

444
Draw funny portraits of each other together.

445
Start a round story where each person adds a word using the first line: *When I was in outer space, I met...*

446
Make a shaving cream ball pit in a kiddie pool.

447
Play parachute using a sheet and jumping off low pieces of furniture.

448
Look through photo albums together or view family slides, movies, or videos.

449
Go to a county fair.

450
Invest in a rock tumbler so you can polish all of the cool rocks your kids find on their outdoor adventures.

451
Make a pasta necklace.

452
Go to the beach.

453
Have a garage sale.

454
Make homemade popsicles.

455
Work on a stamp
collection together.

456
Make an ice bowling set by
freezing water in a balloon and
milk cartons for the bowling
ball and pins.

457
Teach your child how
to ride a bike.

458
Play Cranium.

459
Have a family poker night.

460
Create a family cookbook.

461
On a rainy day bounce
out pent-up energy at a
trampoline park.

462
Play tic-tac-toe Frisbee.

463
Attend a performance
of classical music.

464
Go soda bottle bowling in your
kitchen using empty soda
bottles and an inflatable ball.

465
Go on a bug hunt.

PLAY IS OFTEN AS IF IT WERE A SERIOUS LEARNING. PLAY IS SERIOUS

TALKED ABOUT
RELIEF FROM
BUT FOR CHILDREN
LEARNING.

—Fred Rogers

466

Ride a roller coaster.

467

Play the fortunately/ unfortunately game by starting a story with the word "fortunately." The person who goes next has to continue the story starting with "unfortunately." Keep going back and forth until you run out of ideas.

468

Leave a gift for your delivery drivers.

469

Make handprint leaves and turn them into a festive fall garland.

470

Draw a picture using only your feet.

471

Play shuffleboard.

472

Play TV tag. Just like regular freeze tag, when the person who is "it" tags someone they have to freeze. They can only be unfrozen if another player touches their shoulder and shouts the name of a TV show. Remember, each TV show can only be used once!

473

Make your own "telescope" out of paper towel rolls. Decorate them any way you want!

474
Catch lightning bugs,
then release them and watch
them flicker away into
the night.

475
Go for a canoe ride.

476
Learn to make paper airplanes
together, then race them.

477
Visit an island.

478
Make magazine collages
with recycled magazines, glue,
and card stock.

479
Explore a forest.

480
Catch snowflakes on
your tongue.

481
Dig for fossils by burying toys
in the sandbox or a box of dirt
and having your kids carefully
excavate them. Turn it into a
science experiment by having
them keep a log of what they
found and where the found it.

482
Play the card game spoons.

483
Create your own backyard
splash pad by laying out
a tarp and a sprinkler!

484
Have a fashion show.

Decorate gingerbread men.

Ingredients

1½ sticks unsalted butter, at room temperature
½ cup packed light brown sugar
⅔ cup molasses
1 large egg, at room temperature
1 teaspoon baking soda
1 teaspoon ground ginger
1 teaspoon apple pie spice
½ teaspoon salt
½ teaspoon pure vanilla extract
¼ teaspoon black pepper
3 cups all-purpose flour, plus more for dusting
Frostings of choice, for decoration (optional)
Candies of choice, for decoration (optional)

Directions

- Place the butter and brown sugar in a mixing bowl and beat at low speed with a handheld mixer until combined. Increase the speed to high and beat until the mixture is light and fluffy. Add the molasses, egg, baking soda, ginger, apple pie spice, salt, vanilla, and pepper and beat for 1 minute.

- Slowly add the flour to the mixture and beat until it is a stiff dough.

- Divide the dough in half and wrap each half in plastic wrap. Flatten each piece into a pancake and refrigerate for 1 hour. The dough will keep in the refrigerator for up to 2 days.

- Preheat the oven to 350°F and line two baking sheets with parchment paper. Place the dough on a flour-dusted work surface and roll to a thickness of ¼-inch. Dip cookie cutters in flour and cut the dough into desired shapes. Transfer the cookies to the baking sheets and bake until firm, about 10 minutes.

- Remove the cookies from the oven, let rest for 2 minutes, and then set on wire racks to cool completely. Decorate with the frosting and candies, if desired.

486

Have a family slumber party.

487

Make nature bracelets by wrapping a piece of tape around your wrist and going for a walk in the park. You can add leaves, pebbles, sticks, and other treasures to the bracelet while you explore.

488

Play cornhole.

489

Have a bubble gum bubble blowing contest and see who can blow the biggest bubble without popping it.

490

Visit a botanical garden.

491

Get a butterfly kit and watch the caterpillars grow into butterflies.

492

Have a snowball fight.

493

Go play laser tag.

494

Have a formal dinner with your nicest clothes on.

495

Make a family banner for the living room. Let each family member add to it using whatever craft materials they want. Make sure everyone signs their masterpiece.

496

Take a drive to look at holiday decorations.

497

Trace each family member's hands on a piece of paper, then decorate them however you want to make a big family banner.

498

Make marshmallow snowmen using toothpicks and small pieces of candy.

499

Visit a petting zoo and feed the baby animals.

500

Try skipping double Dutch.

501

Have a water gun battle.

502

Make toilet paper ninjas using toilet paper rolls and markers. Be sure to hide them throughout the house just out of sight like true ninjas!

503

Play on the monkey bars.

504

Make your own bleach t-shirts by taking black tee shirts and putting cardboard inside the shirt between the front and back. Using bleach pens, draw designs on the fabric and let sit for up to 10 minutes. Then, rinse off, wash separately, and dry before wearing.

505

Make beeswax lip balm.

Ingredients

1 tablespoon beeswax, grated
1 tablespoon coconut oil
Raw honey, as needed
2 capsules vitamin E oil

Directions

- Create a double boiler by filling a small pan halfway with water. Then, add a smaller metal bowl to the pan, being sure it does not touch the base of the pan.

- Bring the water to a boil and add the beeswax. Once the beeswax is halfway melted, add the coconut oil and honey and mix together. Add the vitamin E and mix until combined.

- Remove the pan from heat. Once the mixture has cooled slightly, transfer to a lip balm tin or other sealable container. Allow to cool to room temperature before use.

Make hot fudge sundaes.

Ingredients
    1 (11.75 oz.) container hot fudge topping, warmed
    2 pints vanilla ice cream
    Whipped cream, to taste
    ½ cup chopped pecans or walnuts (optional)
    4 maraschino cherries, for garnish

Directions
- Place as much hot fudge as you desire in the bottom of four tulip sundae dishes or bowls.

- Scoop the ice cream into the bowls, then top with more hot fudge.

- Top each sundae with whipped cream, pecans or walnuts (if using), and a maraschino cherry and serve.

507
Declare it "Play Hookie Day" from anything school- or work-related.

508
Watch a movie at a drive-in.

509
Do some apple printing by cutting apples in half (carefully), carving designs into the fruit, and using them to make pictures.

510
Commit to an annual themed trip.

511
Make a weather chart for each day of the week and let your kids predict the weather.

512
Have an art sale.

513
Use tissue paper to create "stained glass" windows in fall shapes. Simply cut out tissue paper into fun shapes and tape onto the windows with double-sided tape.

514
Make a giant boardgame in your backyard.

515
Get a book of riddles. See if you can stump each other. Then, try writing your own riddles.

516
Roast pumpkin seeds.

517
Visit an art museum.

518
Play the card game Set.

519
Create a family
workout routine.

520
Play man hunt. This is like
hide-and-seek but reversed.
One person goes and hides,
while everyone else tries to
find them. If the hider makes it
back to a designated starting
area without being found, they
win! The first person to find
the hider gets to hide next.

521
Go sailing.

522
Have a watermelon seed
spitting contest.

523
Play Risk.

524
Make moccasins together.
Most craft stores have kits you
can buy for all shoe sizes.

525
Build an easy swing
from a plastic box and some
heavy-duty ropes.

526
Play hangman.

527
Work together on
a model kit.

Bake strawberry shortcake.

Ingredients
   2 lbs. strawberries, hulled and halved
   ¼ cup granulated sugar, plus 2 tablespoons
   2 cups all-purpose flour, plus more for dusting
   2 teaspoons baking powder
   ½ teaspoon lemon zest
   ¼ teaspoon cinnamon
   1½ cups heavy cream
   Whipped cream, to serve

Directions

- Preheat the oven to 400°F.

- Place the strawberries and ¼ cup sugar in a large bowl and cover with plastic wrap. Let the mixture sit until the strawberries start to release their juice, about 45 minutes.

- Place the flour, baking powder, remaining sugar, lemon zest, and cinnamon in a mixing bowl and whisk to combine. Add the heavy cream very slowly and beat with a handheld mixer until a smooth dough forms.

- Transfer the dough to a lightly floured work surface and roll it out into a 9 x 6-inch rectangle that is approximately ¾-inch thick. Use a floured biscuit cutter or mason jar to cut six rounds from the dough. Place the rounds on a greased baking sheet, place the sheet in the oven, and bake until golden brown, about 12 minutes. Remove from the oven and let cool for 10 minutes.

- Starting at the equator, cut each of the cakes in half. Place a dollop of the whipped cream on top of one of the halves, followed by a few scoops of the strawberries and their juices. Top with the other half and serve.

527
Play jumbo Jenga.

530
Set up a glow-in-the-dark ring toss using glow necklaces or bracelets as rings.

531
Make up your own tongue twisters.

532
Hold marble races using an old pool noddle. Just cut the pool noodle in half, then race the marbles down the centers to see whose marble is fastest.

533
Carve a watermelon like you would a pumpkin to make a summer jack-o'-lantern.

534
Ride a carousel.

535
Make a front door wreath using fake pine needles or silk flowers.

536
Stay at a local hotel overnight.

537
Make butterflies from coffee filters and clothes pins. Simply decorate your coffee filter however you'd like, then gather in the middle and pin with a clothes pin. You can even decorate the clothes pin, if you'd like.

538
Play musical chairs.

539
Take a night hike.

540
Play "I spy" during a
nature walk.

541
Stuff leaves into orange
trash bags and decorate them
like pumpkins using paint,
markers, or anything
else you'd like.

542
Play the rhyming game
by going in a circle and having
one person say a word, then
the next person has to
come up with a rhyme
in 10 seconds or
they're out.

543
Have an International
Holiday Day, where you serve
food from and learn about
different cultural celebrations.

544
Watch the sunrise together.

545
Learn about Cinco de Mayo
and how celebrating defining
moments in history can help
bring people together.

546
Put up a tent and have a
backyard campout.

547
Visit a local bookstore.

ADULTS
FOLLOW PATHS.

CHILDREN EXPLORE.

—Neil Gaiman

548
Count the satellites that pass in the night sky and talk about space.

549
Make a care package to send to a relative who lives far away.

550
Shop at a thrift shop.

551
Make your own photo booth, complete with cut-out masks and funny backgrounds. You can set up a camera on a timer or even use your computer as the photography station.

552
Make hand-painted t-shirts with puffy fabric paints.

553
Have an egg toss.

554
Play the name game, but with favorite foods, songs, books, etc. to see how well you know your family! Simply create a circle of family members and pass a ball back and forth. Before passing the ball to someone, however, you have to yell something about them (their favorite song, for example). See how fast you can get the ball going!

555
Go paddle boarding.

556
Play Frisbee golf.

557

Set up a spy scavenger hunt for your kids. Be sure to have them sneak around to avoid being "caught."

558

Go to a $1 movie.

559

Learn about Yom Kippur, why many different cultures fast, and about the importance of asking for forgiveness when you've done something wrong.

560

Build a rope ladder for a tree on your property to make a hangout spot.

561

Join your kids for lunch at their school, if possible.

562

Ride a bus until you feel like getting off. Explore wherever you end up and then get on the same bus line and head back home.

563

Play mancala.

564

Create a family book, with information and pictures about each family member.

565

Have a water balloon fight.

566

Play balloon volleyball.

567

Play bingo.

568

Make homemade slime.

Ingredients

1 (8 oz.) bottle Elmer's white school glue
Food coloring (optional)
1 tablespoon baking soda
1½ to 2 tablespoons contact saline solution, plus more as needed

Directions

- Add the glue and food coloring, if using, to a bowl. Stir until the desired color is achieved. Then, mix in the baking soda.

- Add 1½ tablespoons saline solution and mix. If the mixture is still too sticky, add additional saline solution in ½ tablespoon increments.

- Once the mixture has reached the desired texture, knead until the slime forms together. It will start out sticky and slowly reach the desired consistency. If the mixture is still too sticky, add more saline solution as needed. Store in an airtight container.

Play ghost in the graveyard.

How to play:

- Choose one player to be the ghost. Designate an area as home base. Have the ghost run and hide while the rest of the players count to 100.

- Have all of the players go in search of the ghost. Meanwhile, the ghost's goal is to jump out and tag a player without being seen. If a player sees the ghost and hasn't been tagged, they should shout "Ghost in the graveyard!" as loud as they can and run back to base.

- Anyone who has been tagged becomes a new ghost and goes with the first ghost to hide and try and tag everyone. The game ends when everyone has been tagged.

570

Go for a wagon or sleigh ride, depending on the season.

571

Build a robot out of empty boxes of all shapes and sizes.

572

Make a bird feeder using an empty 2-liter bottle, two wooden spoons, and string. Drill two holes in the bottle big enough for the spoons to go through, making the holes slightly bigger on the end where the spoon head will be. Attach the string to the cap of the bottle, fill the bottle with birdseed, and place the spoons through the holes. The seeds should fall out onto the spoons.

573

Make jewelry out of recycled objects.

574

Play foursquare.

575

Go to Disney World or Disney Land as a family.

576

Create a balance beam or tightrope between two trees just a few inches off the ground and take turns balancing.

577

Take an empty picture frame out with you when you visit the park and have a family photo shoot.

578
Help teach your older kids how to drive down a dirt road or in an empty parking lot.

579
Be a tourist in your own town.

580
Visit an arcade.

581
Play with shaving cream and food coloring.

582
Go for a dog sled ride.

583
Have a craft day using things you find at the dollar store.

584
Play Clue.

585
Make a painter's tape racetrack and race toy cars around your living room.

586
Play lacrosse.

587
Have a donut breakfast at the park.

588
Put on old shoes and go for a stroll in a stream.

589
Go curling.

590

Make a pie with freshly picked berries.

Ingredients
1½ cups fresh blueberries
1 cup fresh blackberries
1 cup fresh raspberries
1½ cups fresh strawberries, washed and tops trimmed, and halved
1 tablespoon fresh lemon juice
½ cup light brown sugar
2 tablespoons cornstarch
2 premade pie crusts
½ cup unsweetened raspberry preserves
Whipped cream, to serve

Directions
- Preheat oven to 375°F.

- In a large bowl, toss the berries with the lemon juice, brown sugar, and cornstarch. Transfer the mixture to a large saucepan and cook over medium heat for about 3 minutes, until the fruit starts to warm and break down.

- Working with the crust in a 12-inch cast-iron skillet, scrape the fruit and resulting juices onto the crust.

- In a small bowl, stir the preserves until slightly liquefied. Drizzle over the pie.

- Put the skillet in the oven and bake for about 30 to 40 minutes until the filling is bubbling.

- Remove the skillet from the oven and allow to cool before serving. Serve with fresh whipped cream.

591
Play Qwitch.

592
Make stepping-stones for your garden with footprints and handprints using plaster of Paris. You can even add decorative elements like colored glass stones or buttons.

593
Visit national monuments.

594
Make ice sculptures by freezing blocks of ice and "carving" them into unique shapes using hot water.

595
Go downhill skiing.

596
Make a domino chain reaction together.

597
Play freeze dance.

598
Have dessert out at a restaurant one night.

599
Go 24 hours without internet, TV, or your phone.

600
Have a PJ party.

601
Make clothespin people using clothespins, markers, scraps of fabric, and glue.

602
Tour a factory.

603
Go to or organize a swap meet.

604
Blow a dandelion and make
a wish together.

605
Play sea monster by lying
in the shallow end of the pool.
Move yourself using only your
hands and try and chase down
the other swimmers. This
works best if you can hold your
breath for a while and "attack"
swimmer's ankles.

606
Bob for apples.

607
Paint the sidewalk with water.
See how fast the sun makes
your art disappear.

608
Make pinwheels using squares
of paper, brass fasteners,
and straws. Simply take the
squares of paper and fold in
half to make a triangle shape,
then unfold and fold the other
direction to make another
triangle. Cut halfway along the
folds on each edge, then punch
a hole in one corner of each
of the cut triangles. Fasten the
four corners in the center with
a brass fastener, push through
the middle of the paper, and
press the fastener through the
straw. Open the fastener to
finish the pinwheel.

OTHER THINGS
BUT WE
END WITH

MAY CHANGE US, START AND THE FAMILY.

—Anthony Brandt

Whip up homemade aqua sand.

Tools
Wax paper
Play sand
Fabric protector
Clear vase or bowl
Water, as needed

Directions
- In a well-ventilated space, lay out the waxed paper and place the sand on top.

- Spray the sand with fabric protector, mixing the sand together between sprays until all of the sand has been fully saturated. Allow to rest until dry, about 1 hour.

- To use, fill a clear vase or bowl with water and drizzle the sand into the water to create cool shapes and textures.

Make your own cloud dough.

Ingredients
8 cups all-purpose flour
1 cup vegetable oil
Oil-based or powdered food coloring (optional)

Directions
- Divide the flour into 4 bowls, with 2 cups of flour per bowl.

- Divide the vegetable oil into ¼ cup sections and mix with food coloring of your choice.

- Add each ¼ cup vegetable oil to a separate bowl of flour and mix by hand until combined. Keep in a flat storage bin between uses.

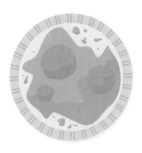

611
Play Settlers of Catan.

612
Create a timeline of your family history.

613
Play foosball.

614
Have a water balloon baseball game using a bucket of water balloons and old towels for the bases. Make sure to use a plastic bat!

615
Play the card game slapjack.

616
Listen to classical music.

617
Watch Sunday football as a family.

618
Make a lemonade stand.

619
Go to all the parks within a 10-mile radius and pick out your favorite. If you're feeling ambitious, you can even make "park passports" for each person to write down facts about their favorite park.

620
Play Pictionary.

621
Get some pots and pans for drums, dress up, and have a parade.

622
Create a new family tradition and follow it every year.

623
Do a ropes course.

624
Play in the sandbox together.

625
Build a goal box together and take out one goal every week and try and do it together. This can include things like, "spend more time as a family" or, "learn how to play the piano."

626
Play hopscotch.

627
Learn to play the harmonica.

628
Visit a farm.

629
Make your own trail mix together. Feel free to add traditional things like nuts and pretzels, as well as fun options like M&Ms or yogurt-covered raisins.

630
Start an ant farm.

631
Play indoor baseball. Set up three paper plates as the bases, then use a crumpled-up paper ball to pitch and "bat" with your hands.

632
Make an at-home taco bar.

633

Make no-bake cookies.

Ingredients

1½ cups granulated sugar
¼ cup honey
½ teaspoon salt
½ cup whole milk
1 stick unsalted butter
¼ cup unsweetened cocoa powder
3 cups old-fashioned rolled oats
1 cup creamy peanut butter
1 teaspoon vanilla extract

Directions

- Combine the sugar, honey, salt, milk, butter, and cocoa powder in a saucepan and cook over medium heat. Once everything is combined, cook for an additional 1 to 2 minutes.

- Remove the saucepan from heat and stir in the oats, peanut butter, and vanilla extract. Let cool for two minutes.

- Line a baking sheet with parchment paper. Use a tablespoon to scoop the cookies onto the baking sheet. Place in the refrigerator and chill for an hour before serving.

Play reindeer games.

Tools
Fake reindeer antlers
Red noses (optional, but recommended)
Plastic or paper rings

How to play:
- The object of this game is to get as many rings on the reindeer's antlers as possible before time runs out. One player wears the antlers and nose, while their teammate tries to toss the rings onto the antlers.

- Mark a spot at least 5 feet away and have the antler-wearing player take their spot. The reindeer can try and help catch the rings, but they should not move any closer to the player and cannot use their hands. The team with the most rings on their reindeer wins!

635

Decorate bikes and have a neighborhood parade.

636

Have a wheelbarrow race. Be sure to pair kids together if they are about the same size.

637

Make some Shrinky Dinks. You can find Shrinky Dinks at most craft stores, just make sure you do a test to see how much the pictures will shrink beforehand.

638

Play truth or dare.

639

Have a family Pokémon card tournament.

640

Play twenty questions.

641

Have a water cup race where you see who can get to the finish line first without spilling a cup of water filled to the brim. For older kids, make it harder by having them balance the cups on their head or having them walk backward.

642

Make a slideshow of your favorite digital photographs.

643

Create your own popcorn songs by having one person sing a line, and the next person sing the next line. The more ridiculous the better!

644

Throw a Valentine's Day party.

645

Play Xactika.

646

Have a coloring book party complete with gel pens, markers, colored pencils, and more.

647

Get a snow cone maker and make snow cones. You can cut down on the amount of sugar by using sugar-free juice instead of traditional syrups for a refreshing summer treat.

648

Make a terrarium with air plants, sand, and mason jars.

649

Make marshmallow and toothpick sculptures together. For the aspiring architect, try to make a working bridge using only marshmallows and toothpicks.

650

Play sharks and minnows in a pool.

651

Build a toothpick bridge or building using only toothpicks and a hot glue gun.

652

Make a list of the coolest tourist attractions within a day trip of your home and visit them.

Make your own rock candy.

Tools
4 mason jars
Cotton thread
4 pencils

Ingredients
2 cups water
4 cups granulated sugar
2 drops of food coloring of choice (optional)

Directions
- To begin, clean 4 glass mason jars with warm water. Cut 4 lengths of thread a few inches higher than each jar and tape each thread to a pencil. Wind the thread around the pencil until the thread dangles 1 inch from the bottom of the jar.

- Wet each thread with water and roll in granulated sugar. Set aside to dry.

- Add the water to a medium saucepan and bring to a boil. Add the sugar one cup at a time, stirring between each addition. Continue to stir, while boiling, until all of the sugar has been added and has completely dissolved. Remove the pan from heat.

- If using the food coloring, add to the mixture and stir until the syrup has a nice, even color. Allow to cool for 10 minutes.

- Pour the sugar syrup into each jar. Then, lower the string into the jars and set the pencil across the top.

- Place the jars in a dark, quiet place and cover with plastic wrap or paper towels. The crystals should begin to form after 2 to 4 hours. If nothing has taken hold after 24 hours, you may need to repeat the recipe again.

- Once the rock candy has reached the desired size, remove, allow to dry, and serve.

654
Jump in leaves.

655
Have everyone start on the same page of Wikipedia, then tell them what page they need to get to by only clicking links in each article. Whoever finds the shortest way to the final page wins.

656
Iron leaves between two sheets of waxed paper and hang them in the window.

657
Try a free project at a local craft or hardware store.

658
Go ice fishing.

659
Write and produce a play to perform in front of other family members.

660
Build a leaf fort.

661
Have a masquerade party at your house, complete with masks and dancing.

662
Plant flowers for bees.

663
Make a spring garland using coffee filters painted to look like flowers.

664
Have a juggling contest.

665
Draw a picture of your house from the outside.

666
Attend a barn dance.

667
Go on an overnight backpacking trip.

668
Make wind spinners from old juice cartons by cutting a square out of the front of each side of the carton and folding it so they all face the same direction. Color them however you want and hang them on the porch to watch them spin.

669
Play volleyball.

670
Set up recycling bins and a recycling system for your household.

671
Act out your favorite Disney movies from memory.

672
Go tobogganing.

673
Visit the oldest house in your town.

674
Have a thankfulness circle where each person says what they're thankful for.

675
Go for an ATV ride.

THE INFORMALITY

A BLESSED

ALLOWS US ALL TO

WHILE LOOKING

OF FAMILY LIFE IS
CONDITION THAT
BECOME OUR BEST
OUR WORST.

—Marge Kennedy

676

Go walking in the mall before the stores open.

677

Make a no-sew blanket using two pieces of fleece fabric. Cut into each side, making strips that are about 1 inch wide and 4 inches long but are still attached at the center of the fabric. Then, tie the edges of the pieces of fabric together to make your new blanket.

678

Gather the family to enjoy a story podcast.

679

Have a backward day. Wear your clothes backward, have breakfast for dinner, and even try talking backward!

680

Ride a Ferris wheel.

681

Build a water blob. Using painter's tarps, tape all but one side of a tarp together using Duct Tape. Then, fill the blob with water and tape off the last side. Let your kids jump on the blob all they want and remember that the more water that leaks out the better!

682

See who can build the tallest tower using blocks or Lego bricks.

683

Have a classic video game night where you play arcade games like Pac Man or Space Invaders together.

684

Have a lazy day where you order takeout and everyone stays in their PJs all day.

685

Make tie-dye shirts. You can get your own tie-dye kits from the store, just make sure to invest in lots of gloves!

686

Strap on some life vests and kayak on a lake.

687

Make homemade Valentine's Day cards.

688

Play pop the balloon by jumping on balloons and seeing who can pop the most.

689

Have a backyard bonfire.

690

Celebrate National Pancake Day (September 26) by having a pancake bar, complete with all kinds of fun toppings.

691

Record yourselves acting out a play.

692

Make a bat house. Many woodworking stores offer bat house kits, or you can make your own using Popsicle sticks.

693

Clean up trash at a park in your neighborhood.

Bake apple cider donuts.

Ingredients

1½ cups apple cider
2½ cups granulated sugar
5 tablespoons unsalted butter, at room temperature
2 large eggs, at room temperature
3½ cups all-purpose flour, plus more for dusting
1¼ teaspoons salt
2 teaspoons baking powder
1 teaspoon baking soda
3½ tablespoons ground cinnamon
½ teaspoon grated nutmeg
½ cup buttermilk
1 tablespoon pure vanilla extract
Canola oil, for frying

Directions

· Place the apple cider in a saucepan and bring to a simmer over medium-high heat. Cook until the cider has reduced to approximately ⅓ cup. Remove from heat and let cool completely.

· Place 1 cup of the sugar and the butter in the mixing bowl of a stand mixer and beat until the mixture is pale and fluffy. Add the eggs one at a time and beat until completely incorporated before adding the next one.

- Place the flour, salt, baking powder, baking soda, ½ teaspoon of the cinnamon, and nutmeg in another mixing bowl, whisk to combine, and set the mixture aside.

- Add the buttermilk, cooled reduced cider, and vanilla into the bowl of the stand mixer. Add the flour mixture and beat on low speed until combined.

- Generously dust a work surface with flour and place the dough on it. Pat it into a rectangle that is ¾ inch thick. Sprinkle the dough generously with flour, transfer to a parchment-lined baking sheet, cover with plastic wrap, and place in the freezer for 20 minutes.

- Remove the dough from the freezer and use a floured biscuit cutter or mason jar to cut it into rounds. Place the doughnuts on another parchment-lined baking sheet and place them in the freezer for 5 minutes.

- Place the remaining sugar and cinnamon in a bowl, stir to combine, and set the mixture aside.

- Add canola oil to a Dutch oven until it is 3 inches deep and heat it to 350°F. Working in batches of three doughnuts, place the doughnuts in the hot oil and fry until golden brown, about 1 minute. Turn the doughnuts over and fry for another minute. Transfer the cooked doughnuts to a paper towel-lined plate to drain.

- When the doughnuts are still warm but cool enough to handle, dredge them in the cinnamon-and-sugar mixture and serve immediately.

675
Play superhero.

676
Have a subway adventure.

697
Write letters to out-of-town relatives or friends and send them through the post office. Make sure to let the kids lick the envelopes!

698
Dig for worms.

699
Make a rope swing and hang it from a tree.

700
Go to a hockey game.

701
Do a puzzle.

702
Play sardines by having one person hide and everyone try and find them. However, once someone finds them, they have to quietly join the hider in their hiding place until only one person is left not "sardined" into the hiding place.

703
Have a crab walk race.

704
Head to a tree farm and pick out your own Christmas tree.

705
Play Banana Grams.

706

Make a family phone book full of important phone numbers.

707

Stay in a cabin.

708

Celebrate New Year's Eve and discuss how different cultures celebrate the new year in unique ways.

709

Have a splash fight while you're swimming.

710

Turn April Fools into an all-day (fun and kind) prank contest. The person who pulls the most successful pranks gets to pie a parent.

711

Do a secret act of service for someone in your family.

712

Memorize the capitals of countries or states and see who can list the most without stopping.

713

Play Sorry!

714

Have an arm wrestling contest.

715

Choose a map of an area near you and mark off all the exciting places you want to visit.

716

Make homemade salt play dough.

Ingredients
1 cup salt
1 cup water
½ cup flour, plus more as needed

Directions
- Combine the salt, water, and flour in a medium saucepan and cook over medium heat. When the mixture is thick and rubbery, remove from heat.

- Once the mixture is cool enough to handle, knead in additional flour until the dough is easily pliable. Store in an airtight container when not using.

717

Make your own caramel corn.

Ingredients
12 cups freshly popped popcorn
Carmel, to taste, warmed

Directions
- Place the popcorn in a large bowl and drizzle the caramel over the top. Toss until the popcorn is evenly coated.

- Pour the popcorn onto a parchment-lined baking sheet in an even layer. Let stand for 30 minutes before serving.

718

Plant a butterfly or hummingbird garden.

719

Have a family pet fashion show.

720

Talk about sustainability as a family and see if you can go waste-free for a whole day, or even a whole week if you're up for a challenge.

721

Create a house of cards.

722

Play shaving cream Twister by adding shaving cream mixed with food coloring to each of the dots.

723

Play ultimate Frisbee.

724

Create an obstacle course outdoors and have a race.

725

Play tennis with clean fly swatters and balloons.

726

Take turns explaining a film plot badly while everyone else has to guess what movie you're referencing.

727

Play with sand toys and trucks in a sandbox.

728

Go whitewater rafting.

729
Visit an escape room together.

730
Mix soda flavors at a local convenience store, then swap sodas and have each person guess what the mixture is.

731
Play checkers.

732
Make a birthday flag for an upcoming birthday.

733
Build the biggest prank machine ever.

734
Have a race by hopping on one foot.

735
Go on a frog-finding adventure. Be sure to let them go after you catch them!

736
Watch reruns of old shows that were popular when you were young.

737
Play tetherball.

738
Make a map of your neighborhood and include illustrations of each house. This is a great way for younger kids to learn their home address.

739
Visit a kids' science center.

Make a sensory aquarium jar.

Tools

    Mason jar with lid
    Sand
    Water
    Blue food coloring (optional)
    Glitter (optional)
    Glycerin
    Ocean-themed toys
    Glass rocks (optional)
    Super glue or hot glue gun (optional)

Directions

- Clean out the mason jar with hot water and dry thoroughly. Add some sand to the bottom of the mason jar.

- In a separate container, mix together some water and blue food coloring, if using. Add the glitter and a few drops of glycerin and stir. Once mixed, set aside.

- Add the toys and glass rocks, if using, to the bottom of the mason jar.

- Pour in the water until it almost reaches the top of the container.

- Screw on the lid securely, and, if worried about the jar being opened, glue shut using super glue or a hot glue gun.

741

Make chocolate-covered strawberries.

Ingredients
- 1 pint fresh strawberries
- 1 cup semi-sweet chocolate chips

Directions
- Wash the strawberries and pat them dry.

- Line a baking sheet with parchment paper.

- Place the chocolate chips in a microwave-safe bowl and microwave on high for 25 to 35 seconds. Remove from the microwave and mix until smooth. Dip each strawberry into the chocolate halfway, or completely, if you prefer.

- Place the strawberries on a baking sheet and place in the refrigerator for at least two hours before serving.

  Tip: Jazz up your strawberries by covering them in nuts, coconut, or small candies while the chocolate is still soft.

742

Go surfing.

743

Make corn on the cob prints using fresh corn on the cob and washable paints. Be sure to lay down newspaper first, as things can get messy.

744

Play basketball.

745

Schedule a professional family photo shoot.

746

Ride a train.

747

Volunteer at a food kitchen or homeless shelter.

748

Play zombie tag. Choose one person to be the zombie, while everyone else tries to run away. The zombie cannot run and has to walk around like a zombie. Once a "human" gets tagged, they also become a zombie. Whoever is the last human standing wins!

749

Try your hand at canning.

750

Make stress balls using rice, balloons, and a funnel. Simply funnel the rice into an uninflated balloon and tie it off at the end for an easy stress reducer.

751

Go for a family bike ride.

752
Make swords out of rolled up newspaper and have a pretend sword fight.

753
Play HORSE.
Determine who goes first by playing rock-paper-scissors. The first person takes a shot at the hoop, adding whatever tricks they want (shooting with their eyes closed, behind their back, with one arm, etc.). If they make the shot, whoever is next in the order has to copy them exactly. If they miss, they get a letter from the word "horse." Keep going until only one person still has letters left. For younger kids, set up a mini basketball net next to the real one and make sure to keep the tricks easy!

754
Make snow angels.

755
Start a family YouTube channel.

756
Learn about Hanukkah and the importance of celebrating good things that have happened in history, as well as coming together as a family to brighten spirits and celebrate your culture.

757
Have an "animal race" where everyone has to walk like a different animal.

758
Play dress-up.

HAVING
GO IS HOME.
TO LOVE IS FAMILY.
BOTH IS

SOMEWHERE TO HAVING SOMEONE AND HAVING A BLESSING.

—Unknown

759
Play duck, duck, goose.

760
Tell your child three things you really like about them.

761
Whittle utensils, toys etc. from wood you find outside or in the recycling bin. This is best done with older kids.

762
Celebrate Star Wars Day (May 4) by dressing up like Jedi (or Sith) and having a "lightsaber" fight with pool noodles.

763
Lie on a blanket and look for shapes in the clouds.

764
Play ping-pong.

765
Make paper chains to decorate your house or child's room. For a fun recycling project, make the chains out of old magazines.

766
Go roller skating.

767
Pair off into teams and draw blindfolded portraits of each other, then hang your masterpieces for every- one to enjoy.

768
Write stories together, then read them out loud as a family.

769
Have a jumping contest.

770
Play two truths and a lie. Each person goes around in a circle and says two true things and one lie. Everyone else guesses on which thing they said is the lie. The people guessing each get a point if they guess the lie correctly. The person lying gets a point for each person they fool with their lies. Whoever has the most points after you go around the circle wins.

771
Visit a haunted house.

772
Make homemade gifts for members of your family.

773
Have an indoor picnic.

774
Bake your favorite bread recipe together. Be sure to enjoy it warm with plenty of butter or jam!

775
Collect leaves and then try to identify them by researching them online or at your local library. Then, turn your leaves into a scrapbook complete with notes on each kind of leaf.

776
Make a pinecone bird feeder.

777
Play wiffleball.

778

Make chocolate and walnut fudge.

Ingredients

1 cup chopped walnuts
¾ lb. quality bittersweet chocolate, chopped
2 oz. unsweetened barker's chocolate, chopped
1 stick unsalted butter
2 cups granulated sugar
1 teaspoon pure vanilla extract

Directions

- Preheat the oven to 350°F and line a square 8-inch cake pan with heavy-duty aluminum foil so that the foil extends over the sides. Spray the foil with nonstick cooking spray.

- Place the walnuts on a baking sheet, place it in the oven, and toast the walnuts for 5 to 7 minutes, until lightly browned. Remove from the oven and set the nuts aside.

- Place the chocolates and the butter in a heatproof mixing bowl and set aside. Place the sugar in a deep saucepan and cook over medium heat until it has dissolved and is boiling.

- Continue to cook, while stirring constantly, until the sugar reaches 236°F. Pour the sugar over the chocolates and butter in the mixing bowl. Whisk until smooth and then stir in the toasted walnuts and vanilla.

- Spread the fudge in an even layer in the cake pan. Refrigerate until the fudge is set, about 2 hours. Use the foil to lift the fudge out of the pan and then cut the fudge into squares.

179

Splatter paint together. Be sure to wear old clothes and lay down newspaper.

180

Celebrate National Hugging Day (January 21) with lots of hugs. If you have someone in your family who doesn't like hugs, don't worry, you can always give out Hershey's Hugs instead.

181

Hunt for constellations.

182

Create sock puppets together. You can use hot glue to add things like googly eyes, yarn hair, and more to old socks. Just make sure to use clean socks!

183

Go see Santa during the holiday season.

184

Play ball tag. This is just like normal tag, except the person who is "it" has to tag people by throwing a ball at them. Be sure not to use a hard ball!

185

Build a toy car racetrack out of old boxes, paper towel rolls, and other repurposed materials. You can even make a whole car town complete with garages and a mechanic, if you're feeling adventurous!

186

Make a family first-aid kit and talk about home safety.

187
Find shells at the beach together.

188
Make toilet paper roll snowmen using white paint, markers, and scraps of paper for the scarf and hat. You can use toothpicks for the arms, if you'd like.

189
Draw a masterpiece on the sidewalk with chalk.

190
Create a family handshake.

191
Paint with squirt guns on a canvas. Be sure to do this activity outside!

192
Play pool together.

193
Blow bubbles.

194
Take a garden gnome with you on all your summer adventures and take photos of the gnome doing activities alongside your family. At the end of the summer, create a scrapbook full of the gnome's photos.

195
Attend a local parade, or maybe even have your own float!

196
Cook a meal together.

Make milkshakes.

Ingredients
2 pints vanilla ice cream
½ cup whole milk
½ teaspoon salt
2 teaspoons vanilla extract
Mint, for garnish (optional)

Directions
- Place all of the ingredients, other than the mint, in a blender and puree until combined.

- Pour the milkshakes into tall glasses and, if desired, garnish with mint.

798

Make colorful eggs for each season and be sure to display them.

Ingredients
Boiling water, as needed
Vinegar, as needed
Food coloring of choice
12 eggs, hardboiled

Directions
- Mix ½ cup boiling water, 1 teaspoon vinegar, and 10 to 20 drops food coloring into a cup, then mix. Repeat for all desired colors.

- Dip the eggs into the dye and allow to sit for about 5 minutes. Remove carefully using a slotted spoon or tongs, then allow to dry.

799
Jump in a bouncy castle.

800
Rearrange the furniture in your kids' bedrooms. Make sure to have your kids draw out their master plan before you start reorganizing.

801
Donate to a food bank as a family.

802
Create your own nature notebook.

803
Hold a recycling contest. Whoever can collect the most recycling over the course of a week wins.

804
Paint garden sticks for your potted plants or family garden.

805
Play Apples to Apples.

806
Create your own sandbox using an old storage bin and sand.

807
Play octopus tag. Like normal tag, designate one person to be "it." Once the person who is "it" tags someone, they have to sit down where they were tagged and attempt to also tag people without standing up or moving from where they are sitting. Whoever is the last person tagged is "it" next.

808
Fly a kite.

809
Create a home version of a popular game show.

810
Visit an amusement park.

811
Watch a tree specialist cut down a tree.

812
Pretend to be on a cooking show and have everyone make a dish using specific ingredients. Then, serve the resulting feast for dinner.

813
Play pinball.

814
Play loud music and dance crazy.

815
Have a read aloud night.

816
Get ice cream from an ice cream truck.

817
Play Hula-Hoop ring toss, using buckets as the posts. You can also divide into teams and have one person act as the post while the other person tries to toss Hula-Hoops over them.

818
Make peppermint bark together using your favorite recipe.

OHANA MEANS
FAMILY MEANS
LEFT BEHIND

FAMILY AND NOBODY GETS OR FORGOTTEN.

—Lilo & Stitch

819
Start a happiness jar by writing down what makes you happy and then picking one happy thing to read off every day.

820
Watch a fireworks show.

821
Play hide-and-seek in the dark with glow sticks.

822
Go on a whale watching trip.

823
Memorize the periodic table of elements together.

824
Hide plastic Easter eggs for an impromptu egg hunt at any time of the year.

825
Create your own holiday and celebrate it each year.

826
Clean the house together.

827
Spend the day at a waterpark.

828
Make glow-in-the-dark mason jars by putting glowsticks in mason jars and placing them around the house.

Make apples out of pipe cleaners and string them together to make a fall garland.

Create secret messages using a mirror to write backward.

Have a backyard circus.

Roast marshmallows over a campfire and make s'mores.

Create your own Summer Olympics, complete with tinfoil medals, of course!

Create paper plate apples using paper plates, a stapler, and markers, then use them to decorate your kitchen for the fall.

Make a kid-sized hot air balloon by covering a hamper in fabric. Then, either blow up a ton of balloons and tie them together or purchase a large number of helium balloons. For helium balloons, gather them into a large bundle and tie them together, then tie to the edges of your hamper. For regular balloons, tie them together and perch over your hamper using dowels and tape.

Make your own homemade bouncy balls.

Ingredients

2 tablespoons warm water
½ teaspoon borax
1 tablespoon glue
1 tablespoon corn starch
Food coloring (optional)

Directions

- Set aside two plastic cups. Pour the water and borax into the first cup and stir using a disposable stirrer until dissolved.

- Pour the glue, cornstarch, and food coloring, if using, into the second cup, and mix together. Add ½ teaspoon of the borax mixture into the second cup.

- Allow the borax mixture to sit for 15 seconds, then stir. Once the mixture becomes difficult to stir, pour out of the cup and roll using your hands to form a ball. Store in an airtight container when not using.

Bake lemon poppyseed muffins.

Ingredients

1 stick unsalted butter, at room temperature
¾ cup granulated sugar
2 eggs
1 cup sour cream
3 tablespoons lemon juice
1⅔ cups all-purpose flour
1 teaspoon baking soda
1 teaspoon salt
2 tablespoons poppy seeds

Directions

- Preheat the oven to 350°F. Line muffin tins with paper liners.

- In the bowl of a stand mixer, cream the butter and sugar until smooth. Add the eggs one at a time. Scrape the sides of the bowl down well and mix the batter until smooth.

- Add the sour cream and lemon juice. Mix until combined.

- Add the dry ingredients and the poppy seeds. Mix until the dry ingredients are just incorporated. Don't overmix.

- Scoop the batter into prepared muffin cups and bake for 18 to 20 minutes, or until a toothpick inserted into the center comes out clean.

838
Build a lean-to.

839
Have a snowman building contest.

840
Make a pretend grocery store.

841
Celebrate International Talk Like a Pirate Day (September 19) by turning your favorite songs into pirate versions, or by reading pirate stories.

842
Make a stop motion film.

843
Cheer on a family member in a sporting event.

844
Make a family flag and display it.

845
Learn to ballroom dance.

846
Have a holiday or winter movie marathon. Here are a few suggestions to get you started:
Elf (2003)
Frozen (2013)
Rudolph the Red-Nosed Reindeer (1964)
Santa Claus is Coming to Town (1970)
How the Grinch Stole Christmas (1966)

847
Have a family meal outside.

848
Have a $5 shopping day.

849
Visit a firehouse.

850
On masking tape, write
5 silly ways to throw a ball.
You can include things like
through your legs, with your
eyes closed, etc. Tape each
silly option onto separate balls
and start a catching circle.
When you get the ball, you
have to throw it to the next
person the way it says.

851
Make a daisy chain together.

852
Go to a candy store together.

853
Play dodge ball
(use a very soft ball).

854
Make a gingerbread replica
of your house using the
gingerbread recipe
on page 114.

855
Make a tote bag out of
Duct Tape. Simply take a
large piece of paper, fold it in
half, and tape along the sides,
leaving the top open. Then,
cover the rest of the paper
with tape and add Duct
Tape handles.

856
Build a village using blocks,
Lincoln Logs, or Legos.

WHEN ALL THE

AND ALL THE

THE THINGS THAT

FAITH, FAMILY,

DUST IS SETTLED
CROWDS ARE GONE,
MATTER ARE
AND FRIENDS.

—Barbara Bush

857
Have a candy treasure hunt.

858
See how many rounds you can sing of "Down by the Bay" without repeating the added lines.

859
Play monkey-in-the-middle.

860
Have a three-legged race.

861
Paint with toy cars using washable paints. Make sure to do this outside for easy cleanup!

862
Go for a hayride.

863
Play croquet on the lawn.

864
Learn to juggle.

865
Go to a carnival.

866
Have the ultimate night out by going to one restaurant for appetizers, then a new one for your main course, and then finally go somewhere else for dessert. This can work with fast food runs as well.

867
Explore your town on foot.

868
Have a trivia night.

869
Play Battleship.

870
Build a Rube Goldberg machine together to complete a simple task, like turning off an alarm.

871
Paint each other's faces.

872
Plan a one-on-one date with your child.

873
Host a murder mystery dinner.

874
Learn new jokes and have a comedy hour.

875
Try out new restaurants together.

876
Learn a new craft as a family.

877
Start a burn-your-regrets New Year's tradition where you each write down something you didn't like about the past year and then carefully burn them to signal a new year full of fun traditions.

878
Take a cooking class as a family.

879
Roll down a hill.

Make your own oat bars for your next hike.

Ingredients
¾ cup milk
1 cup granulated sugar
¼ teaspoon sea salt
1 teaspoon pure vanilla extract
1 oz. dark chocolate, melted
½ cup creamy peanut butter
⅔ cup quick cooking oats
¼ cup old-fashioned rolled oats

Directions
- Place the milk, sugar, and salt in a small saucepan and whisk together. Cook over medium heat until the mixture thickens and comes to a boil, approximately 10 minutes. Remove the pan from heat.

- Add the vanilla, chocolate, and peanut butter to the pan and mix until well combined. Fold in the oats and mix until completely coated.

- Line an 8 x 8-inch baking pan with parchment paper and pour the contents of the saucepan into it. Press into an even layer and let the bars sit for 30 minutes. They should be firm and not break when picked up. Cut the bars into small sections and serve immediately, or store in the refrigerator.

  Tip: You can always adjust recipe by using half as much honey to replace the sugar.

881
Play Monopoly.

882
Plant sunflowers and keep a growth chart to track how tall they grow.

883
Write letters to Santa together.

884
Have a pun contest.

885
If you live somewhere cold, make your own snow with boiling water. This should only be done by adults. When the temperature outside is at -22°F (-30°C), throw boiling water into the air. The boiling water will turn into snow in midair!

886
Put together your own book of family jokes.

887
Visit a city.

888
Make paper bag puppets using markers, string, and anything else you want!

889
Watch a local live sporting event.

890
Grab a blanket and have a picnic lunch outside.

891
Paint using flowers as your paint brushes.

892
Take a karate class.

893
Visit a retirement home and read stories to the residents.

894
Make a solar system mobile using bouncy balls, markers, coat hangers, and hot glue. You can cut rings out of construction paper for Saturn, too.

895
Create a "Story of My Life" scrapbook.

896
Make a flower crown out of mini daisies.

897
Go to a demolition derby. Expect to see some major crashes!

898
Visit a corn maze.

899
Press summer flowers, then make a pressed flower picture by gluing them to waxed paper.

900
Play the card game war.

901
Trace a tree pattern by placing a piece of paper on the trunk and rubbing a colored pencil over it.

Make a dessert pizza.

Ingredients

5 tablespoons unsalted butter, at room temperature
½ cup caster sugar
1 egg
1 cup self-rising flour, plus more for dusting
Seeds of ½ vanilla bean
1 ball premade pie crust dough
2 tablespoons vanilla pudding
1 royal gala apple, cored and sliced into thin half-moons
1 tablespoon dark brown sugar
1 handful cotton candy (optional)
2 tablespoons spreadable caramel, warmed

Directions

· Preheat the oven to 425°F.

· Place the butter and sugar in the mixing bowl of a standard mixer fitted with the paddle attachment. Beat on medium for 1 minute, add the egg, and beat for another minute. Scrape the mixing bowl as needed.

· Add the flour and vanilla seeds, reduce the speed to low, and beat for 1 minute. Raise the speed to medium and beat until the mixture is well combined.

· Place the dough on a lightly floured surface and roll it into a 10-inch circle that is approximately ½-inch thick. Transfer the dough to a greased pizza pan or baking sheet, spread the butter-and-sugar mixture over the dough, and then gently spread the vanilla pudding on top.

- Distribute the apple slices and sprinkle them with the brown sugar. Place the pizza in the oven and cook until the crust is golden brown, 12 to 15 minutes.

- Remove from the oven, slice into eight pieces, and place the cotton candy in the center, if using. Drizzle the caramel over the pizza and serve.

903
Donate old blankets and towels to an animal shelter.

904
Play the card game liar-liar.

905
Go bowling.

906
Visit a pond and feed the ducks. Be sure not to feed them bread, as bread is bad for ducks (and most birds).

907
Play dominos.

908
Have a stuffed animal birthday party, complete with cake!

909
Build a tree house.

910
Go on a sound walk and see how many different things you hear.

911
Write an autobiography.

912
Have a living room moon landing with cardboard space suits.

913
Freeze small toys in trays full of water, then, once frozen, have a hairdryer race to see who can melt the ice the fastest!

914
Build an indoor golf course.

915
Play cribbage.

916
Build a tower out of couch cushions and pillows and see if you can make it touch the ceiling.

917
Have a dance party.

918
Learn a new word every day for a month.

919
Have a family movie night complete with popcorn.

920
Make grave rubbings of cool tombstones and then use them to decorate for Halloween.

921
Visit a waterfall.

922
Have breakfast for dinner, or vice versa!

923
Visit an archery range.

924
Blow bubbles in really cold temperatures to see them freeze.

925
Have a read-a-thon.

FAMILY IS A

THE STORMY

LIFE JACKET IN SEA OF LIFE.

—J.K. Rowling

926

Make a soda bottle volcano.

Tools
    2 teaspoons dish soap
    ⅓ cup cold water
    1⅔ cups white vinegar
    Food coloring (optional)
    1 (2-liter) soda bottle
    Baking soda slurry (fill a cup ½ of the way with baking soda,
    then fill the rest with water)

Directions
- Combine the dish soap, water, vinegar, and food coloring,
  if using, in the empty soda bottle.

- Mix the baking soda slurry until it is a liquid, then pour the
  slurry into the bottle and quickly step back!

927

Make fondue.

Ingredients
1 lb. Gruyère cheese, grated
½ lb. Emmentaler cheese, grated
½ lb. Gouda cheese, grated
2 teaspoons cornstarch
1 garlic clove
1 cup chicken broth
1 tablespoon lemon juice
Salt, pepper, and grated nutmeg, to taste
Bread or crackers of choice

Directions
- In a bowl, toss the cheeses with the cornstarch until the cheese is well-coated.

- Cut the garlic clove in half. Rub the inside of a crockpot or fondue pot with the garlic, then add the chicken broth and lemon juice and bring to a simmer over low heat.

- Add the cheese mixture all at once. Using a wooden spoon, stir over medium-low heat until the cheese is melted and smooth, about 5 to 10 minutes.

- Season with salt, pepper, and grated nutmeg. Dip your favorite snacks into the fondue and enjoy.

928
Attend a tree lighting ceremony.

929
Make a "laser" obstacle course in a hallway using yarn. This is great for kids who love to play spy!

930
Go to the store and have everyone pick out their favorite type of candle, then take turns lighting them.

931
Have a Nerf gun fight.

932
Go night swimming.

933
Learn Morse code.

934
Make hats out of Duct Tape by cutting a piece of paper into two triangles, taping the two smaller sides together, and then covering the surface with Duct Tape. For more adventurous creators, try and see if you can make a Duct Tape top hat!

935
Have your kids write a letter to their favorite musician.

936
Let your kids make their own fresh orange juice for breakfast.

Teach your kids how to play chess, then hold your very own chess tournament.

Rent a paddle boat.

Have a shelf cleaning day where you donate old books to your public library.

Pretend to be an alien and have your kids explain everyday objects to you in detail. This is a great way to teach them about order of events by having them "teach" you how to make a sandwich with you following their instructions literally.

Go bird watching and keep notes on all the birds you see or hear.

Visit a planetarium.

Pick up a kid-friendly mystery book and try and solve it before the main character does.

Have a stripes and polka dots clothes day.

Make melted crayon artwork by gluing crayons to a canvas and using a hair drier to create cool patterns.

Make and enjoy hot chocolate.

Ingredients

1 cup heavy cream, chilled
½ cup granulated sugar, plus 1 tablespoon
¼ cup cocoa powder
Dash of salt
⅓ cup hot water
4 cups whole milk
¾ teaspoon vanilla extract

Directions

- To make the whipped cream, put the heavy cream into a large bowl and beat on high speed until peaks just start to form. Add the 1 teaspoon sugar and continue beating until stiff peaks form. Put the bowl in the refrigerator while you make the hot chocolate.

- In a medium saucepan, stir together the sugar, cocoa, and salt. Add the water and stir to combine. Cook over medium heat, stirring constantly, until the mixture comes to a boil. Boil and stir for about 2 minutes. Add the milk, stirring constantly until heated. Do not let the mixture come to a boil. Remove from heat and add the vanilla. Pour into mugs and top with fresh whipped cream.

Make pom-poms.

Tools
Rectangular piece of carboard
Scissors
Yarn (bulky preferred)

Directions

- Take the carboard and cut a section, starting at the bottom middle, that is about ½ inch wide and goes up ¾ of the way up the cardboard. You should have a shape that looks similar to a pair of high-waisted pants.

- Wrap the yarn around both "legs" of the cardboard in one continuous motion. Do not weave through the legs. Once you have a large amount of yarn wrapped around the legs, cut the end of the yarn.

- Using a second piece of yarn, tie a knot around the wrapped yarn, using the top space and bottom edge of the carboard you cut to thread the second piece of yarn through.

- Tie off the wrapped yarn as tightly as possible and remove from the carboard. It should look a little like a bow tie.

- Tie the yarn again in the same direction, pulling tighter as you go. Repeat this step two or three times.

- Using the scissors, cut the yarn where it loops around the edges. Fan out the cut yarn to finish the pom-pom.

948

Have a favorite color contest where each person tries to find as many items as they can that are their favorite color. Or switch things up and have each family member find another family member's favorite color!

949

Have your kids write a letter to their favorite children's book author.

950

Use white crayons and paint to make cool contrast drawings. This is especially fun if you use black paper.

951

Play an active video game together, like a dancing game or a sensor-based sports game.

952

Have a staring contest.

953

Go to your kids' favorite playground and join them playing on the swings.

954

Pair off into teams. Each person should draw their teammate as their favorite character from a movie, TV show, or book. Hang all of these pictures up for everyone to view when they're done.

955

Go to your favorite restaurant and have your kids pick out what their parents should eat for dinner (within reason, of course).

956

Make gift baskets for your local retirement community or hospital.

957

Have your kids pick out their favorite famous artists, then have everyone try and draw in the same style as those artists. You can even frame your pictures and have an "art museum" in the living room.

958

Take turns acting out your favorite fairy tales—in costume, of course!

959

Visit your local historical society and see what your street used to look like a hundred years ago.

960

Explore local walking trails as a family.

961

Go to your local store and buy the funniest sunglasses you can find, then take a family photo together.

PEACE IS THE

IT IS SUNSHINE.

OF A CHILD, THE

THE JOY OF

TOGETHERNESS

BEAUTY OF LIFE.
IT IS THE SMILE
LOVE OF A MOTHER,
A FATHER, THE
OF A FAMILY.

—Menacheim Begin

Bake cinnamon rolls.

Ingredients

- All-purpose flour, for dusting
- 1 (26.4 oz.) package frozen biscuits
- 2 teaspoons cinnamon
- ¾ cup dark brown sugar, firmly packed
- 4 tablespoons unsalted butter, at room temperature
- 1 cup confectioners' sugar
- 3 tablespoons half-and-half
- ½ teaspoon pure vanilla extract

Directions

- Preheat the oven to 375°F. On a flour-dusted work surface, spread the frozen biscuit dough out in rows of 4 biscuits each. Cover with a clean dishcloth and let sit for about 30 minutes until the dough is thawed but still cool.

- Combine the cinnamon and brown sugar in a small bowl. When the dough is ready, sprinkle flour over the top and fold it in half, then press it out to form a large rectangle (approximately 10 x 12 inches). Spread the butter over the dough, then top with the cinnamon-and-sugar mixture.

- Roll up the dough, starting with a long side. Cut into 1-inch slices and place them in a lightly greased cake pan.

- Place in the oven and bake for about 35 minutes, until the rolls are cooked through in the center. Remove from the oven and allow to cool slightly.

- Make the glaze by combining the confectioners' sugar, half-and-half, and vanilla in a small bowl. Drizzle over the warm rolls and serve.

963

Make sticky note murals by coloring on sticky notes and arranging them to make a masterpiece.

964

Buy cheap canvas shoes and decorate them together using fabric paints or tie-dye.

965

Get together all the markers in the house and roll out a large piece of paper. Let your kids test all of the markers to see if they have dried out or not, then display the resulting artwork.

966

Play go fish.

967

Learn how to use simple looms to make your own hats, scarves, and more, then donate the results to your local charity.

968

Play Parcheesi.

969

Purchase a ton of pet toys and supplies and donate them to your local animal shelter. Make sure to pick up some rodent and bird supplies as well!

970

Keep a quote book full of the funny or insightful things your kids say, along with the date and how old they are.

Visit your local theater on a throwback movie night.

Design costumes for your kids' favorite stuffed animals or toys, then hold a toy fashion show complete with music.

Make your own personalized license plates for your family bikes or scooters.

On your next vacation, have your kids draw their favorite activities, then put them all together in a scrapbook for your next trip.

Create a dictionary of "family-isms" that only your family says, then ask your extended family to add their own.

Have each family member write down one thing they want to learn over the course of a month, then have the entire family learn along with them.

Have a kindness morning where each family member leaves sticky notes with positive messages on each other's doors for a nice wakeup surprise.

Make a solar oven.

Tools
1 cardboard pizza box
Scissors
Aluminum foil
Clear tape
Plastic wrap
Black construction paper
Newspapers
Ruler or wooden spoon
Thermometer

Directions
- Cut a flap in the lid of the pizza box using the scissors, leaving about an inch between the sides of the flap and the edge of the lid. Fold the flap so it stands when the lid is closed.

- Cover the inner side of the flap with aluminum foil and tape in place. Seal the opening in the box from the inside with a double layer of plastic wrap, with the flap outside of the plastic wrap.

- Line the bottom of the box with the construction paper. Roll up sheets of newspaper and place along the sides of the box to act as insulation. Tape them in place.

- To use your solar oven, place whatever you would like to cook inside the box on a glass plate and close the box. Set your box in direct sunlight with the aluminum angled to reflect onto the food, using the ruler or wooden spoon to prop the hatch open. Cook until done, using the thermometer to check the temperature as it cooks.

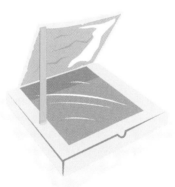

979
Go tide pool exploring.

980
Make your own nighttime activity space outdoors, complete with solar-powered night-lights and lanterns, and allow each kid to add something that represents them to the space.

981
Play Guess Who.

982
Join a beach cleanup as a family.

983
Play marbles together.

984
Have a stay-up-late night on a weekend where the kids can stay up as late as they want (within reason) and just spend time together as a family.

985
Start a button collection.

986
Have a day where you all wear the same color.

987
Play Twister.

988
Try to make the longest paperclip chain ever.

989
Have a sack race.

990
Play Frisbee.

991
Have a "character day"
where everyone pretends to be
their favorite movie or book
characters for the entire day,
complete with costumes.

992
Play a game of touch football.

993
Visit the circus.

994
Go for a hot air balloon ride.

995
Go boogie boarding.

996
Paint terracotta pots and
plant your favorite flowers
or succulents in them.

997
Sing karaoke.

998
Have a rap battle and have
each family member pick out
their own rapper name.

999
Run (or walk) a 5K.

1000
Build an igloo.

1001

Make homemade treats for the family pet.

Ingredients

1½ cups oat flour, plus more for dusting
1½ cups brown rice flour
1 teaspoon baking powder
1 egg
½ cup chicken broth
Smooth peanut butter, for filling

Directions

- Preheat the oven to 350°F. Combine all of the ingredients except for the broth and peanut butter. Slowly add the broth, mixing until the dough forms. If it is too dry, add more broth, if it is too wet, add more flour.

- Roll the dough out onto a lightly floured surface until it is ¼ inch thick. Use a round cookie cutter to cut circles in the dough. Place a small amount of the peanut butter between each round, then gather the edges together to create a small bundle.

- Line a baking sheet with parchment paper and add the treats, keeping them about ¼ inch apart.

- Bake for 25 to 30 minutes or until golden brown. Transfer to a wire rack and allow to cool completely. Store in an airtight container in the refrigerator or give to your furry friend immediately.

THERE'S ONLY
MORE PRECIOUS
AND THAT'S WHO

ONE THING
THAN OUR TIME
WE SPEND IT ON.

—Leo Christopher

About Cider Mill Press Book Publishers

Good ideas ripen with time. From seed to harvest, Cider Mill Press brings fine reading, information, and entertainment together between the covers of its creatively crafted books. Our Cider Mill bears fruit twice a year, publishing a new crop of titles each spring and fall.

"Where Good Books Are Ready for Press"

Visit us online at
cidermillpress.com
or write to us at
PO Box 454
12 Spring St.
Kennebunkport, Maine 04046